The Paradox of Happiness

The Paradox of Happiness

Finding True Joy in a World of Counterfeits

René Breuel

KIRKDALE PRESS

The Paradox of Happiness: Finding True Joy in a World of Counterfeits

Kirkdale Press, 1313 Commercial St., Bellingham, WA 98225
KirkdalePress.com

Print ISBN 9781683592617
Digital ISBN 9781577995326

Lexham Editorial Team: Abigail Stocker, Danielle Thevenaz, and Elizabeth Vince
Typesetting: ProjectLuz.com

For Sarah

Contents

Introduction

When our firstborn son, Pietro, was three months old, my wife and I introduced him to one of our favorite sports: people watching. We walked toward the sunset and emerged at the top of Piazza di Spagna, a 138-step stairway always crowded with people ready to see and be seen. We could view almost all of Rome from the top—the tall, picturesque trees, a few candlelit restaurants, a convent by the hill, upscale shops, and church domes all the way to Saint Peter's across the river.

But nothing was as amusing as watching people march up and down the stairways as if the stairs were their own world-stage runway. The prize for the most elegant person went to a lady in her sixties, who was flowing down the stairs holding hands with a couple of grandchildren, wearing a brown skirt, a beige blouse, and a collar of pearls. The most entertaining scene came from Bengalese salesmen offering fake Gucci and Louis Vuitton purses, who ran away when the police arrived, hid behind a wall, then came back the next minute only to repeat the process again and again. Meanwhile, a couple was exchanging gazes and brushing one another's hair, and a bride-to-be rang a bell and walked among the crowd sheepishly while her girlfriends laughed and took pictures.

Then we introduced Pietro to the nations—and stereo-types—of the world. The most Japanese group had latest-model cameras hanging from each of their necks. The most Brazilian couple was wearing, fittingly, Brazilian soccer jerseys. The most American person, though not easy to spot at first, was unmistakable when found: moustache, tight jeans, and cowboy hat. Not that Sarah and I were any more fashionable. She had borrowed one of my pullovers, which was on the brink of being downgraded to the pajama category, and my shirt was sprinkled with the vomit Pietro had poured over me an hour before.

It was then that someone stood out from the crowd. It was a girl in her twenties, apparently from eastern Europe or Russia. She was dressed as if for an evening cocktail, with elaborate makeup. Her hair was as spotless as if she were in a shampoo commercial. She was taking pictures with several poses and looks, so we figured she was a model. But as we observed more closely, we noticed that the photographers were not of the usual kind: they were her mom and her little sister. They were following the model-to-be, taking pictures perhaps for her first portfolio, which would appear on the desk of some agency among several thousand other young ladies' pictures vying for a dim light of attention.

That girl was striving for something the rest of us on those stairways also secretly wanted: to be noticed, to feel that we were savoring life and that we were happy. We were all there to enjoy a gelato with a view, but we also fostered the hope that being part of this postcard would somehow satiate our inner hunger. We too wanted pictures to be taken of us and to feel that we transcended the multitude. Tourists or locals, fashionable or not, we were all watching the human spectacle and examining every clue for the arrival of happiness.

I looked down to Pietro. He was drinking his baby milk with closed eyes, absorbed in his own world. I felt like saying, "When your heart becomes restless, when you come to seek something higher and long for joy, Piazza di Spagna is not the place to come, nor any other piazza, runway, stadium, or shopping mall."

Where to go? Who to listen to? Some of the greatest thinkers in history have written about the good life. Their reflections, arising from humanity's manifold traditions, have produced rich cumulative wisdom. In my view, however, one of these thinkers stands out. Many add nuances; a few provide understanding; one unveils the key for true contentment. The fact that this thinker has been historically understood in religious terms does not bar unbelievers from his insights. On the contrary, it is additional motivation to investigate the vision of life that made so many adore him so much. No matter our background or current state of belief, we can all benefit from the teachings that have changed countless lives and made communities across the centuries and continents bloom.

In this book, we will examine Jesus' counterintuitive call to happiness. The fundamental Christian reflection on happiness appears in some of Jesus' most avoided words—words we sometimes skip when we read the Gospels and that preachers prefer not to cover, but words that shine with truth and overflow with life. Mark 8:34–35 presents the greatest of Jesus' paradoxes—the moment when Jesus focuses his teaching on the art of living in two sentences that are so poignant and surprising, but also so countercultural and paradoxical, that they make us look at the page again and ask, "Did Jesus really mean this?" In this crucial passage, Jesus teaches us that it is by losing and giving that we have life. If we live as Jesus invites us to, as the universe around us pulsates, as our own hearts long for, we shall be deliciously happy. But it will happen as a great paradox, for we receive life by losing it. We get by giving. We find joy when we stop worrying about it. We flourish when we help the people around us flourish.

The first part of this book, "The Drama of Modern Happiness," analyzes the trajectories of our current models of happiness. The way we understand fulfillment has taken a specific shape over the centuries. Happiness has come to be equated with pleasure, divorced from the ethical texture of life, and wrapped in pretty items for consumption. Our quest for happiness now follows commercial, skeptical, even imaginary paths, but these paths reveal the fundamental self-centered orientation of our lives and the bent-in, curved nature of our souls. Yet this posture is not the way we were created, nor is it the key to fulfillment and joy.

Part Two explores Jesus' paradox in Mark 8:35: "For whoever wants to save their life will lose it, but whoever loses their life for me and for the gospel will save it." We will discover the relevance of this paradox for the dynamics of happiness, for when we forget about our well-being and live for things other than ourselves, we are surprised by happiness knocking unexpectedly on our door. It comes as a consequence of an open, outward-facing posture—as a by-product of being interested and immersed in life. Only when we transcend the prison of the self can we enlarge our hearts to savor the full breadth of life's delights. Happiness follows a selfless attitude that gives of itself instead of being centered on the self. We find happiness when we stop searching for it. We achieve when we give up. We find when we look elsewhere.

Part Three, "The Rhythm of the Liberated Life," investigates how we come to live Jesus' paradox of happiness: with the great invitation he extends to us in Mark 8:34 to deny ourselves, take up our crosses, and follow him. More than obtaining anything, what we long for above all else is to give of ourselves, to present ourselves to one another, and to be embraced. We are happy when we manage to transcend our ego and move out of ourselves. In the final analysis, the measure of our satisfaction is the measure not of how much we get, but how much we give.

Ready for this paradox?

Happy are the people who work for the happiness of others.

PART ONE
The Drama of Modern Happiness

CHAPTER 1
Plastic Happiness

Coming home one day, I saw a billboard picturing a slim girl in a spring dress. She was smiling and looking upward, surrounded by light and calm. Next to her were the words, "Happiness is to wear a size-small dress." I felt tempted to go to the nearest department store, ask for the ladies' floor, find a size-small dress, and try to fit into it. I would have to stretch the dress to its limits. I am not the muscular type, but I'm pretty sure I don't fit into a size-small dress either. Surely I would draw some suspicious looks if I opened the curtain and emerged into the fitting area, limping in a miniscule dress, to see myself in the mirror. Only the song "Macho Man" would be missing to complete the scene. I could not help but feel eager to evaluate my happiness based on that billboard's definition.

No one needs to mention how mistaken that definition is. Not only does it exclude the wonderful male half of humanity (I can almost hear a roar of protest from bars and stadiums everywhere), but it also hurts the feminine hearts that know they cannot meet that unrealistic standard. The majority of women, who do not fit in a size-small dress, feel diminished, unattractive, and unworthy. The few ladies who do fit in it feel pressured to keep their slim waistlines while wondering why don't they feel happy from it. All of us ask: Really? It *that* happiness?

As harmless as it might seem, that billboard definition is part of a culture that defines beauty and happiness according to its own commercial logic. It is an illustration of our society's ideal of happiness as duty—as an implacable, unbinding rule forced down on everyone. "Everyone should and must be happy," we hear, "or something is wrong." Happiness has been made such an unquestionable norm that people worry if they do not feel bliss every day, and "they become unhappy for not being happy."[1] The breeze of enjoyment becomes a burden and a responsibility. And if happiness becomes a duty, and someone fails this duty—as we all do—happiness becomes guilt, and lack of happiness is ostracized. This is a notion of happiness that is anything but happy.

OUR HUNGER FOR HAPPINESS

Happiness as duty is one of our current distortions of the ideal of happiness. But behind this caricature lies a basic human truth: we all want to be happy. "Happiness" is the word we use to name the basic state we want to achieve in life. We wish to be well, to have peace, to be liked. We want comfortable days filled with pleasure and not with pain. We want meaning and purpose. We want to love and be loved, to have our best moments last forever. Whatever term we use, happiness is the central drive of our lives and the governing concept for our ambitions, desires, and motives.

"All look for happiness without exception," wrote Blaise Pascal. "Although they use different means, they all strive toward this objective."[2] People take different paths—some looking for happiness in a lifetime of meaningful work, some in intimate love, some in intense pleasures, some in easy moments—but all aspiring to the same end: a content life. Happiness may be measured by dollars, hugs, or naps, but it is always pursued. In Pascal's words, "So this is the motive for every deed of man, including those who hang themselves."[3] Or, as Alexander Pope eulogizes,

> Oh, happiness, our being's end and aim!
> Good, pleasure, ease, content! Whate'er thy name:
> That something still which prompts the eternal sigh,
> For which we bear to live, or dare to die.[4]

The sheer controlling force that the idea of happiness exerts upon our lives can sometimes be surprising, for we tend to focus instead on achieving the things we believe will make us happy. We conceive stepping stones that mark the way toward happiness, and we focus more on these steps than on the idea of happiness itself. We think so much of the career path needed for professional recognition, for example, that often we do not ask if professional recognition will make us happy at all. Or we work hard to build a secure financial life but fail to question the link, if there is one, between financial security and happiness. But happiness is what we look for with these pursuits. An astute observer of humanity such as Sigmund Freud could not have concluded otherwise:

> What do men show by their behavior to be the purpose and intention of their lives? What do they demand of life and wish to achieve in it? The answer to this can hardly be in doubt. They strive after happiness; they want to become happy and to remain so.[5]

Happiness, however we understand it, is the fundamental human quest.

IS IT OK TO WANT TO BE HAPPY?

This is also the case for Christians—we just use different language. We shy away from words like "happiness," "desires," "pleasure," or "satisfaction" and the inelegant associations they connote. Yet the pursuit of happiness is still what governs our hearts. It may be the reason why we became Christians in the first place: we may have concluded that we would be happier by receiving Jesus' life and salvation. "If I were to ask you why you have believed in Christ, why you have become Christians," reasons Augustine, "every man will answer truly, 'For the sake of happiness.' "[6] We realize that Jesus is the answer for our search. We glimpse Jesus' promise of happiness and understand that he will satiate the hunger of our hearts.

It is all right to want to be happy, by the way, for God created us to be happy. He was the one who put into our hearts this longing for peace and wonder and delight. God is the one who bestows the gift of life for our enjoyment of himself and his creation. "I have come that they may have life, and have it to the full," said Jesus.[7] God's plan for his creatures is a *happy* existence: in harmony with God, one another, and creation; with moments of joy and festivity; savoring the pleasures God scattered over creation; celebrating God's goodness; loving and serving one another.

Happiness is certainly not the governing concept in the Christian worldview, nor should it remain the ultimate reason of life for those who come to know a God more worthy than any other pursuit. In the coming pages, we shall indeed question the central throne that happiness occupies in our hearts. Nevertheless, contentment is valid, legitimate, and desirable. In Martin Luther's words, "We now know, thank God, that we can be merry with a good conscience, and can use God's gifts with thankfulness, inasmuch as he has made them for us and is pleased to have us enjoy them."[8]

More fundamentally, happiness is a valuable Christian quest because it is rooted in God's own being: our God is a happy God. He created the world out of the overflow of his being so that we could participate in his own delight.[9] His joy was too great not to be shared. We long for it because we were created in the image and likeness of a jubilant, party-throwing God. Our aspiration for a happy life is not a desire that displeases him. Rather, it is an expression of our longing for God's blissful life and a hunger for the banquet of blessedness reserved for us in heaven.[10] Happiness names the basic human pursuit, and because it is an attribute of God and the purpose behind God's creation of the world, it is also a worthy Christian ideal.[11]

ARTIFICIAL HAPPINESS

That does not mean, of course, that our current pursuit of happiness is not without problems. Our understanding of a fulfilled life has been distanced from the Christian ideal of life with and in God, and has been trimmed down to something else. The idea of happiness has undergone specific intellectual and cultural developments in the last centuries; currently, it embraces a rather unique, distinctive shape.

For one, we have reduced happiness to the individual realm—from an ideal for collective life, for the flourishing of humanity and loving social relationships, into a private, self-serving pursuit. Happiness has become the result of individual efforts instead of community life. We have also severed the ethical root of the notion of happiness. Instead of being conceived of as a result of virtue, happiness is now thought of as something smaller and trivial—as fragmentary moments of pleasure. A happy life is thought of as a succession of days showered with pleasure and only occasionally sprinkled with pain.

The notion of happiness, as we understand it today, is something individual and momentary. This idea is distant from Jesus' "blessed are the pure in heart" or from Aristotle's definition of happiness as an "activity of the soul expressing virtue."[12] It does not encompass goodness, love, or generosity; neither is it "secured through virtue," as Thomas Aquinas put it.[13] It is the enjoyment of private moments of pleasure.

This cultural understanding has roots in the modern retrieval of the Epicurean philosophy of life, which is based on pleasure and pain. Epicurus taught in ancient Greece that "pleasure is the beginning and goal of a happy life." John Locke helped reintroduce this perspective in the seventeenth century into our mainstream conception of happiness when he said, "*Happiness* then in its fullest extent is the utmost Pleasure we are capable of, and *Misery*, the utmost Pain."[14] Happiness was equated with pleasure. It was detached from the ethical notions of good and evil to be instead attached to the circumstantial concepts of pleasure and pain. A centuries-long marriage that united happiness and virtue as a good life started to crumble before the dazzling rival of pleasure.

With these developments, happiness became not only independent of virtue and ethics. In an astounding reversal, eventually it became the very definition of goodness. Jeremy Bentham popularized utilitarian ethics in the eighteenth century with the maxim: "It is the greatest happiness of the greatest number that is the measure of right and wrong."[15] From this point, a quite specific understanding of happiness became unrivaled in Western culture: happiness as pleasure, happiness as the ultimate aim in life, and thus happiness as the measure of right and wrong. It is no surprise that when a thinker like Freud came to express what happiness consisted of in the twentieth century, the conclusion was: "As we see, what decides the purpose of life is simply the program of the pleasure principle."[16]

This contemporary definition of happiness is rather thin when compared to the more robust, life-encompassing understanding held not too long ago. It is now a free-floating notion—a vaporous, indefinite idea hovering over our heads, unrelated to the texture of our existence that is colored by virtue or the lack of it. Happiness, as we understand it, does not emanate from generous, warm hearts. It is just the product of fortunate circumstances that, by effort or luck, may fall upon someone—that may *happen*. "It is thus very clear that with respect to happiness, good and evil are in themselves indifferent," concluded Julien de la Mettrie, voicing the common assumption of the age. "The one who receives more satisfaction from doing evil will be happier than whoever receives less from doing good."[17] If pleasure is the definition of happiness, we can get a lot of it without a concern for acting rightly. But happiness as pleasure is a much smaller happiness too: It is reduced to some rare, brief moments in an ocean of ordinary life and boredom. It is fragmentary, scrappy, random, minimal happiness.

Our current notion of happiness as individual pleasure is also artificial, since it is divorced from suffering. In fact, it is understood as the *opposite* of suffering—as an endless succession of calm and pleasant moments. But suffering is part of life. We cannot evade it. To exclude suffering from our notion of an ideal life is to hold an artificial notion of happiness. It is to cage happiness in the realm of unreality, for suffering is part of our everyday lives, and it is part of happy moments too. To exclude suffering is to exclude life.

And if happiness is divorced from goodness and suffering, it is also divorced from reality. It is reserved for those who win lottery tickets or collect worshiping fans or have perfect families. It is a conception so removed from reality that it becomes impossible, serving only to haunt and beat down those of us who cannot extend emotional peaks into the infinite nor eliminate every vestige of pain. It is plastic, cosmetic happiness, useful for advertising—even for selling size-small dresses—but not much else.

CHAPTER 2
The Spectrum of Possibilities

Heart-shaped pillows. Teddy bears who send kisses. Movies that exalt the magic of love at first sight. Girls receiving jewel-priced flower bouquets at work. An "I love you more than ever" banner from Jen to Brad in front of your house. That soft, mellow voice on the radio wishing everybody a happy Valentine's Day "from the bottom of my heart."

For romantic folks like me, Valentine's Day is a celebration of romance, enchantment, and intimacy. Let me make clear to starry-eyed sweethearts that last year I bought Sarah a rose (the full bouquet was so expensive!) and prepared her breakfast in bed. (I accept suggestions and ideas for next year.)

But when I see heart-shaped pillows and teddy bears who send kisses, I confess that part of me screams (accompanied by the stomping of feet and pulling out of hair). A tsunami of sugary romance encourages us to think endearing thoughts, carry baby pandas on the bus, and open our chests to Cupid's arrow. Our ears get to hear sensational gossip (like who the cutest guys in the office are) and Matt's (one of the cute guys) plans to propose that evening by hiding the diamond ring inside a chocolate cake to be discovered while a band plays "The Way You Look Tonight." Not to mention those of us who are single and have to sit behind the panda on the bus, enduring giggles and the long kiss in the seat ahead. (Ever thought of taking a Swiss Army knife out of your pocket and discretely removing the eyes of the panda while the kiss goes on?)

Jokes aside, our sugary Valentine's Day is an annual reminder of the offer of consumer happiness. Whether or not we participate in this celebration of romance, and even if we love to receive flowers and buy the teddy bears who send kisses, we all recognize that the image of ideal romance being sold—and the notion of happiness behind it—are quite specific: it is contentment packaged in items ready to be purchased.

How do we react to this artificial notion of happiness glowing before our eyes?

REJECTING ARTIFICIAL HAPPINESS

The first option is to deny the idea of happiness altogether. This is the path of skepticism—of those who do not distinguish the ideal of happiness from its overt plastic representations and who strive to make the best out of ordinary living. It is the attitude of those who mock Valentine's Day as something purely commercial. It is the mindset of those who are happy to wear a dress in size large or medium, and who look down on people who wear size small and feel they are happy because of it.

This option is lucid, for it recognizes the artificial nature of happiness reduced to pleasure and the emptiness of this conception. It questions the false promises of billboards and magazine covers. Ernest Hemingway raised this skeptic banner when he grumbled, "Happiness in intelligent people is the rarest thing I know."[1] Instead of becoming fascinated with consumer culture, people of this posture recognize that happiness can't be bought and that it is not the teddy bear that produces an intimate relationship.

Yet this path does not have the resources to conceptualize an alternative notion of well-being. It finds cracks in the system, but it does not have the platform from which to suggest a viable substitute. When we align with this mindset, we feel mature and superior—judging those who still think that winning the lottery will change their life and make them happy—but we don't have another concrete proposal for happiness. The prescription here is just to grow up, forget the sense of wonder, joy, peace, love, and delight that haunts our hearts, and live decently quiet lives.

Although this option seems to deny the notion of happiness, those who put it into practice find that it is impossible to eliminate the longing for it. They cannot deny happiness altogether—to yearn for it is part of being human—and end up affirming a milder, more realistic vision of a satisfied life. "We don't need to win the lottery," we reason, "but an annual family trip is sensible enough." We turn to justifications to try to explain away our desires for delight and the unhappy existence we still wish was happy.

This path does not question *the way* we search for happiness. Rather, it tries to make the goal more modest and achievable (fit into a medium-size dress instead of a small) or more intelligent or refined (watch independent movies instead of blockbusters, for instance). It eventually redefines happiness into an unassuming, everyday affair—usually as a stable job and a healthy home. It ends up as a low-key redefinition of plastic happiness.

People pursuing this path often have a hazy sense that they are missing out on life. They know that the promises of artificial happiness won't satisfy them, but they feel something great is still missing. They hear Jesus saying that he came that we may have life and have it to the full, but they don't glimpse how this life can take shape and wonder if Jesus was only talking metaphorically.

SURRENDERING TO
ARTIFICIAL HAPPINESS

The second option can often coexist with the first: it is to live under the pressure of commercial happiness and to try to satisfy its demands—sometimes concretely, sometimes in an imaginary way. We perceive that the happiness being sold to us is artificial, but its attraction is so magnetic and constant that we catch ourselves pursuing it with our thoughts and actions.

Epictetus stated, "That which is happy must possess in full all that it wants, must resemble a person who has achieved his fill—neither hunger nor thirst can come near it."[2] We know this is an unrealistic ideal, but it is repeated to us so often that we let our desires and imaginations be molded by the demands of total satisfaction. We turn on the TV and see smiling people and commercials for fascinating products. We arrive at the doctor's office or hair salon, and we find periodicals such as *People* magazine, inviting us to read about people who have perfect moments, lead exciting lives, and are the envy of other gorgeous people. Our minds fly away: *What would* People *magazine write about me?* Or we open a magazine like *Forbes* or *Fortune*, where successful businesspeople share secrets on how to arrive at the top. *What will I say to the folks at the office when my promotion is announced?* we imagine.

This reluctant fascination with artificial happiness is a lucrative alternative. It spans entertainment industries eager to soothe and amuse us—no matter the time of day and or the technology necessary to deliver distracting goods. Artificial happiness is the enticement behind the advertising system too, which stamps in vignettes and magazine covers the life we should and could have if only we buy the products displayed. Self-help literature helps to close the deal, convincing us that the gap between happiness and our current state is just a matter of simple steps. Plastic happiness is the lure that drives much of the modern economy. It is the lullaby that reassures consumer society's ability to sell comfort, pleasure, and meaning in life.

The irony is that the blind quest for pleasure is the surest way to miss the satisfaction we seek. "Most people rush after pleasure so fast that they rush right past it,"³ quips Søren Kierkegaard. The unrealistic expectation of perfect fulfillment taints moments that would be fine and joyous if we enjoyed them with serenity. Marriages and relationships are hurt because we expect too much of them. Our self-image is damaged because we let ourselves believe we are not intelligent or charismatic or interesting enough. Happiness becomes a burden and responsibility, filling with guilt those who cannot achieve ideal standards. The expectation of perfect happiness never becomes concrete; it hovers as a mirage, as an oasis that steers those who seek it to existential drought.

In our struggle to resolve the tension between the lure of happiness and the daily demands of routine, we often develop an imaginary parallel universe—an alternative self. We maintain heroic versions of ourselves in our imaginations—fantasy personae we seek to believe are our real selves, instead of the bland, common people we are in reality. We grow tired of our old, dull selves and imagine the exciting person each of us will be when our ambitions are realized, and with it the thrill of finally being accomplished, recognized, beloved. Our imagination flies away. *My first picture in the profile feature would be with that red tie, books in the background, and a champagne glass in my hand.*

In these daydreams, the pleasures of possibilities far exceed the authenticity of reality. We can forge attractive selves and breathe glamour and comfort. "One must be susceptible to illusions," recommends Marquise du Châtelet, "for it is to illusions that we owe the majority of our pleasures. Unhappy is the one who has lost them."[4] As tragic as this advice may sound, we often drag our bodies through daily routine while keeping our minds busy with a pantheon of fantasies. We dream about the applause we will receive when our pet dream comes true, how we will say wise and charming things, and how we will prove to the world that we are not insignificant after all.

A recent mechanism that gives room to some of our fantasies is social media. Like our own version of *People* or *Fortune*, social media allows us to upload our best pictures and our best sentences to impress friends. We see others with pregnant bellies or smiling in front of the Eiffel Tower, and we imagine how our page will be even more impressive: *I can't wait to see everyone's reaction to my New Year's party photo.* We notice that someone else has a larger list of friends and go in search of popularity: *Let me write my funniest sentence and break the record for the number of comments.*

Our poor selves try to track along the vast horizons of our imagined or virtual selves. They pretend they don't mind bearing the weight of unrealistic demands, of being traded for an attractive ghost, of being discarded for being bland and boring— that is, for being normal and human—and for hiding brilliant fragments amidst a very ordinary life. This goes on until we convince ourselves that we are really extraordinary, that this dull self is not actually us, and that we have not yet had the chance to prove our worth to the world.

Ironically, even if we do achieve our dreams, we will still not find ourselves. Our true selves are not there to be found. We traded a person for a ghost, and when this imaginary self comes true, it does not come true—it vanishes. The excitement, pride, and satisfaction of success are there, and yet they are not. Our achievements feel more like fool's gold: like a treasure deeply longed for but found rather worthless once it is at hand.

This mismatch between what was expected and what comes true leaves us feeling empty in moments of success. Our hunger is not satiated. Weren't we supposed to find ourselves, to uncover our true being, to secure enduring love? No, we were not. We traded in. We chased imaginary selves, and this is the last way of encountering oneself. We dreamt we were awake, but we have not yet opened our eyes.

To deny happiness and redefine it, to chase artificial notions of happiness and imaginary pleasures—none of these paths unearth the happiness we look for. Our society keeps itself locked within these options, sometimes migrating from one to the other, sometimes claiming to find an undiscovered pleasure that will now guarantee our happiness. The attentive observer sees through it all—and despairs.

THE UNDERLYING LOGIC

These paths fail to achieve true happiness because, although they seem substantially different, they are undergirded by one fundamental posture: self-centeredness. However one defines happiness—whether in skeptic, consumerist, or imaginary terms—the pursuit of satisfaction is a self-serving affair. We perform activities that we hope will make us happy. This orientation toward ourselves is the great logic behind our actions, the standard mode of the human heart. It is an assumption so deeply ingrained in our minds that it is hard to imagine life in any other way. How can someone live without having the well-being of the self as the end goal? How can someone pursue happiness by a logic other than self-satisfaction?

But this connection is the central assumption we have to untangle in Jesus' analysis. Achieving happiness is not necessarily linked with the pursuit of happiness. A satisfied self is not the immediate result of successful efforts to be satisfied. Happiness is distinct from self-centeredness; in fact, the two concepts are opposite. And that's why our common paths to happiness fail: They spring from unfulfilled hearts trying to satisfy themselves. They run along the tracks of self-service. If we are to distill a different path to happiness, we can't just fashion a new definition of it or come up with novel milestones of a happy life. We have to investigate the very *way* we function. We have to unearth the most basic dynamics of the heart.

If the diagnosis is superficial, the remedy will be superficial as well. If we switch the search for consumer goods to inner tranquility, self-service may still be the governing logic under which we operate. If we change our ambition of being a rock star to being a renowned physician, adulation may still be the thing we are after. It won't matter how thoughtfully we engineer our definition of happiness or how creatively we conceive objects of interest. The root of our unhappiness lies deeper: in our self-oriented posture to life.

TURNED IN ON OURSELVES

The key observation behind Jesus' alternative for happiness is that we live—obviously, but importantly—for our own sake. This is the rule we follow in our quest for happiness, the logic that runs our lives. How can we best satisfy the self? We are, in other words, bent creatures, people turned in on ourselves. The self is the starting point of our actions; its satisfaction is the end behind our pursuits. We approach life from a center that seeks to rearrange reality around its orbit. As Martin Luther put it, Scripture "describes man as so turned in on himself that he uses not only his physical but even his spiritual goods for his own purposes and in all things seeks only himself."[5] In a similar way, Augustine defined sin not as a substance but as a perversion of the will bent aside from God toward lesser things. He stated that this very "*preference* of its own being and of the knowledge and enjoyment of things temporal, to the one eternal Good … is what constitutes sin."[6]

Let's be clear: to have a self is not the problem, nor is the desire to enjoy the world and to be happy wrong. Rather, sin is characterized by this turned-in-on-itself condition, by a love of self so prevailing that it subordinates other loves and desires, even for God, to itself. Karl Barth describes the human person as "turned in upon himself and finding his satisfaction and comfort in his own ego."[7] The self is the object to which we are bent and to which we want to converge reality around us.

When we function in this way, we domesticate relations to serve our own purposes. The liveliness of the world around us withers behind lenses able to distinguish only the shadows of self-interest. We distort our capacity to see and damage our ability to love, for our relationship with ourselves becomes so predominant that it absorbs other relations into its logic. We chat briefly here, we voice a half-hearted prayer there, but a meaningful, soul-deep connection rarely occurs. Because the self exerts such a gravitational pull, other good ends in life are pulled in to serve and build up the self. We relate to God and to others *for our own sake*.[8] For example, to love someone for the attention they give us is ultimately a love of attention itself; mature love means loving the person and not just the attention they provide.

In the process, relationships may cease to be true relationships—they may become components in our preoccupation with ourselves. People are welcomed less as people in their own right, as a conscious "you," with whom we relate as another invaluable self, to be treated rather as "it"—as a part in our self-affirming mechanisms. Our relationship with ourselves is so intense that it overshadows the attention we try to direct outward.

In other words, sin turns us inward and severs us from others and from God. It inflates our love of the self to the extreme of absorbing all of life into it; or, rather, to the extreme of diminishing all of life to the size of a starving self. The logic of self-love becomes the logic we live by. In this state, Pascal describes that the heart "cannot by its very being love anything else except for selfish reasons and in order to enslave itself, because each thing loves itself more than anything else."[9] We hunch ourselves inward and lose interest in what will not benefit us, rolling ourselves "into a ball like a hedgehog with prickly spikes," as Karl Barth put it.[10] We lose the wondrous sight of reality and relationships; our satisfactions are restricted by our incurved egos; our happiness is confined by our self-centered posture.

A FORGOTTEN ALTERNATIVE

And it is here, out of a conscious look at self-centeredness, that a third option emerges: Jesus' paradox of happiness. It is a vision of life so powerful that it can reshape the logic of our existence. It displaces the quest for happiness from the central throne it occupies in our minds, redirecting our thoughts and affections to a new direction. Happiness is removed from its pedestal as the ultimate aim of existence. It becomes a by-product of correct orientation to life. We do not need to be slaves to the ideal of happiness; nor do we need to deny it; nor do we need to let it rule our imaginations until it divides our personality, yet still miss happiness. There is a higher, truer, and holier path. It emerges out of goodness. It embraces and transforms suffering. And it is deliciously happy.

PART TWO

Jesus' Paradoxical
Alternative

CHAPTER 3
A Paradoxical Call

The professor of rhetoric sat down to evaluate the eloquence of the orator. Ambrose's fame was everywhere. Multitudes flocked to hear his words charged with beauty and wisdom. When Augustine arrived in Milan to meet Ambrose, Augustine was already a promising professor of philosophy and rhetoric. He had left his humble North African village to assume teaching posts in Carthage and Rome. He had debated in public and written books. He could express himself with skill and eloquence. He had met great masters of Platonism and Manichaeism, two of the main philosophies of the time. Now he sat down to examine if this preacher from Milan had something new to teach him about the art of speaking in public.

But Augustine was caught by surprise. Ambrose was certainly an excellent orator, but something else captured Augustine's attention. As Augustine tried to evaluate the manner in which Ambrose spoke, he was amazed by the *content* he communicated. In the *Confessions*, Augustine disclosed,

> I studiously listened to him—though not with the right motive—as he preached to the people. I was trying to discover whether his eloquence came up to his reputation, and whether it flowed fuller or thinner than others

said it did. ... And, while I opened my heart to acknowl-
edge how skillfully he spoke, there also came an aware-
ness of how *truly* he spoke.[1]

The worldview that Bishop Ambrose's lips articulated took
Augustine by surprise. He was startled to find answers to his
spiritual longings in a place he had gone only to learn more
about speaking. Shifting his attention to the meaning of the
words he heard, Augustine moved on to become one of the
greatest theologians of all time.

This experience of surprise, of paradox, molded Augustine's
theology and his manner of expressing it. He acquired rever-
ence before a God greater than what the mind can comprehend
or words can express. Augustine also learned the power of a
paradox to point beyond what the eyes can see.

From that moment on, Augustine was not afraid to use
paradoxes to illuminate something of God's vast being. In the
Confessions, he describes God as "brighter than all light, but
more veiled than all mystery; more exalted than all honor,
though not to them that are exalted in their own eyes."[2] In
another passage, Augustine pours himself out in adoration to
God, using a number of paradoxes to express divine complexity and beauty:

Most high, most excellent, most potent, most omnip-
otent; most merciful and most just; most secret and
most truly present; most beautiful and most strong;
stable, yet not supported; unchangeable, yet changing
all things; never new, never old; making all things new,
yet bringing old age upon the proud, and they know it
not; always working, ever at rest; gathering, yet needing
nothing; sustaining, pervading and protecting; creating,

nourishing and developing; seeking, and yet possessing all things.[3]

PARADOXICAL LIFE

But it wasn't only from his personal experience that Augustine learned the importance of the paradox to illuminate who God is and to explain life. He noticed that the category of paradox was central not only in his life but also in the Scriptures. The New Testament is filled with examples of the paradoxical way in which God acts in us. God's power is made perfect in weakness; his foolishness is wiser than human wisdom; freedom is used for service; inexpressible joy takes place amidst grief and trials; treasure in heaven comes through giving to the poor; rest happens when we take Jesus' yoke.[4] It is not the rich, but the poor in spirit who shall receive the kingdom of heaven; it is the meek, not the self-asserting, who will inherit the earth.[5] God's life reverses our existence right-side-up, assembling our hearts in paradoxical ways so we can receive fullness of life. No wonder the apostle Paul could affirm that our lives are "known, yet regarded as unknown; dying, and yet we live on; beaten, and yet not killed; sorrowful, yet always rejoicing; poor, yet making many rich; having nothing, and yet possessing everything."[6]

To sin, holiness may appear absurd, but that's because sin cannot see beyond itself. It requires untwisting through paradox to help us see the rising splendor of God's way of life.

WHAT IS A PARADOX?

A paradox is a counterintuitive, tension-filled statement that may prove to be true after all. It can sound self-contradictory or absurd, but that is exactly its intent. By disturbing common sense, a paradox startles us to reexamine our way of seeing things. It provokes distracted minds with contradiction, so as to ignite thought, shed light on our previous wrong notions, and generate a fresh apprehension of truth.[7] By pairing two seemingly opposing ideas, a paradox performs a double function: it puzzles and relieves; it upsets and strikes awe; it destroys in order to build again. It is like an explosion in the mind that destabilizes assumed ideas to make way for a new beam of insight. A paradox is truth dressed up as absurdity; it is a mirror through which we can see.

Jesus couldn't better express the truth of Mark 8:35 than by a paradox.[8] How else could he, in a single sentence, deconstruct our existential approach while pointing to his counterintuitive way of life? Jesus had already used paradoxes to describe those who see but do not perceive and who hear but do not understand.[9] He would puzzle his hearers by announcing that the last will be the first, the servant is the greatest, and the humble will be exalted.[10] Jesus had an acute eye for human inconsistency. He used paradoxes to throw these contradictions back at us—to help us reason our way out of existential enigmas. Jesus' paradoxes baffle our twisted souls into a fresh arrangement of life.

JESUS' CENTRAL CALL

Let's reread this passage and examine Jesus' call in its context in the Gospels.

> Then he called the crowd to him along with his disciples and said: "Whoever wants to be my disciple must deny themselves and take up their cross and follow me. For whoever wants to save their life will lose it, but whoever loses their life for me and for the gospel will save it. What good is it for someone to gain the whole world, yet forfeit their soul?" (Mark 8:34–37)

Jesus' words are so dissonant from our modern paradigms of happiness that they make us stop for a moment, shake our heads, and wonder, "Did I really read this? Does Jesus really mean it?" You read correctly, and Jesus means it. He is calling us to deny ourselves, to lay down our lives, so we can find life.

This is a pivotal text in the Gospels. Only this passage and a few other stories appear in all Gospels in some form, and among those, only Jesus' baptism, death, and resurrection have similar prominence. Mark uses these words of Jesus to open the second half of his Gospel: now that the disciples understand that Jesus is the Messiah, Jesus can reveal his cross-shaped destiny and invite his followers to the same path.[11] Similarly, Luke places these words in a key transition, between Jesus' ministry in Galilee and his journey on the way to Jerusalem. Matthew gives this passage equal prominence, also halfway in his Gospel, and John contains this message in a different form.

These poignant words of Jesus follow Peter's confession that Jesus is the Messiah (Mark 8:27–30) and Jesus' first prediction of his death (Mark 8:31–33). This middle point of the Gospel culminates the revelation of Jesus' messianic identity so far, affirmed explicitly now by Peter, and invites disciples and readers to look ahead and join Jesus in the journey to the cross.[12] Jesus' cruciform path shapes his followers' cruciform path.

This exchange Jesus had with his disciples is not only extremely prominent; it is also addressed to everyone around him. Mark stresses that Jesus intentionally calls a crowd to listen to these words.[13] The implication is obvious: This text is not an advanced discipleship lesson; it is an invitation to follow Jesus. It is not a hard saying that we should reserve for very committed Christians who are ready for a call to sacrifice. It is Jesus addressing seekers. It is Jesus' message to saints and sinners, to disciples and doubters, to Christians and non-Christians. It is Jesus' central explanation of what it means to follow him.

A PASSAGE ABOUT HAPPINESS?

An honest reading of this passage, however—or of any other passage in the Gospels—must recognize that Jesus does not directly address what we understand today as happiness. Nowhere do we see Jesus providing a clear-cut definition—"Happiness is ..." The categories of thought Jesus used were not centered on the fulfillment of pleasures, nor did they aim only toward the emotional well-being of the self. A truthful study of the Gospels cannot easily distill an approach with the current conventions of self-help, clear steps, and infallible principles for happiness. That wasn't the worldview of the time, nor that of Jesus.

That does not mean that Jesus had nothing to say about our central human search. On the contrary, he gives us a rich, realistic, and paradoxical view of happiness. The task before us is to ask: Of all that Jesus communicated, which teachings referred to what we understand today as happiness? In which ways does Jesus address this theme?

Jesus' most direct avenue to talk about happiness is what he teaches about *life*. We've already seen Jesus declaring, "I have come that they may have life, and have it to the full."[14] He talked about fullness of life, about abundant life, about life in tune with the Father. On numerous occasions, Jesus mentioned his eternal life—a life which, beyond lasting forever, is joyous, satisfied, serene, and happy. When Jesus met the Samaritan woman by the well, he described his *living* water, which quenches our thirst. There are certainly moments in which Jesus uses the term "life" without including the concept of happiness. But most of the time, if we want to understand what Jesus teaches about happiness, we must observe what he teaches about life.

And it is in Jesus' central teaching about life that we find his most direct reflection about the dynamic of happiness.

LIFE IN ITS FULLNESS

Jesus calls us here to reconfigure the logic of our lives: "For whoever wants to save their life will lose it, but whoever loses their life for me and for the gospel will save it."[15] With these words, Jesus reverses our approach to existence: to save life is not connected to wanting to save it, but instead to losing it. We gain life by losing life. To try to save it is to lose it. The paradox crawls upon us and challenges us to reexamine what saving and losing life means. It takes "the meaning of our words away from us, turning them inside out, forcing us to face the possibility that we should fear what we have always wanted and should do what we have always feared."[16]

With this paradox, Jesus invites us to ponder the meaning of the word "life." In a real sense, he's alluding to the basic New Testament truth that we cannot save our souls by ourselves—only Christ can save us. For the early martyrs who faced the threat of execution, for example, the choice for eternal life was not to try to save their earthly life but to lose it, literally, "for me and for the gospel." Losing earthly life for Jesus resulted in saving it for eternity. To rely on one's own efforts and righteousness, to try to save one's life, meant not saving the soul, but losing it.

But I believe Jesus is also hinting at a deeper truth of existence here. He does not refer only to the fact that the final outcome of one's soul depends on reliance upon oneself or upon him. To save life by losing it is not only a truth of eternal destiny. Jesus' paradox also addresses the very *logic* of our existence. After all, Jesus is not talking here to a group of martyrs minutes away from execution. He is talking instead to his disciples, who will follow him for decades, and to the multitude. John Stott emphasizes that, "although Jesus may have had the possibility of martyrdom in his mind, the universal nature of his call ('if anyone') suggests a broader application."[17] Indeed, Luke underlines the day-to-day nature of Jesus' call by adding "daily": "Then he said to them all: 'Whoever wants to be my disciple must deny themselves and take up their cross daily and follow me.' "[18]

Can it be that Jesus uses the term "life" here in a broader sense than just eternal life? Can it be that he refers also to his abundant life? Can it be that Jesus is using the time's terminology to refer to what we today may call really living, being happy? I believe that this is not a paradox about death but about abundant life; it is a paradox not about how to die, but about how to live. Jesus does not present a dichotomy between life on earth and eternal life. Instead, he confronts the *logic* of our lives: it is by giving that we receive; it is by losing that we save life; it is by sharing that we can be full.[19]

This paradox illuminates the form in which Jesus' abundant life takes shape in us. And included in its paradoxical logic lies also Jesus' brilliant observation about happiness. As the whole of his life takes place in a surprising way, so does happiness. We receive when we give; we are happy when we live for God and not for ourselves.

Let's examine this paradoxical logic of life and discover how Jesus reveals the unexpected arrival of fullness of life.

CHAPTER 4
The Gift of Happiness

Small Time Crooks is a Woody Allen comedy that tells the story of an amateur band of bank robbers. Allen's character, nicknamed Brain, conceives a not very original plan to rent a store near a bank, dig a tunnel under the ground, and emerge right in front of the bank's vault. He gathers some fellow unskilled criminals, and they start digging the tunnel while Allen's wife runs a storefront cookie shop. The tunnel digging is a disaster—they run into a pipe and flood the basement with water; they read the map upside down and end up in a fitness store. But the cookie business does quite well, actually. People line up in this little shop for the best cookies in town. As word spreads, multitudes come, the shop receives media coverage, and soon a cookie empire is built. The band of criminals gets unexpectedly rich, but from an honest cookie business.

Life throws some interesting surprises at us. Every now and then a door of opportunity flings open right when we are busy working at something else. Often we are so engaged in a long-dreamt project that we almost miss the surprises that walk by. For example, the most renowned violins in the world (the type of violin that Sherlock Holmes used to play in his books) were the product of a frustrated violin player. Antonio Stradivari worked hard to become a master violinist, but as he grew disappointed at his own limited talent, he discovered that he was quite good at making violins. His seventeenth-century handmade pieces were unequaled for a long time, even by industrially designed violins. A mediocre violin player became a master violin maker.

THE ELUSIVE SEARCH FOR HAPPINESS

The dynamic of happiness may be the greatest pun life throws at us. We do everything in our reach to find happiness, but when the expected moment arrives, happiness does not come with it. Then, in unpretentious moments, in the midst of daily life, when we are thinking about anything but our happiness, we stop for a moment and notice that we feel happy. Happiness arrives as a surprise, as a joke, as a paradox. And it is here that the first part of Jesus' paradox addresses us: "For whoever wants to save their life will lose it" (Mark 8:35).

What do we understand by saving life, enjoying it, being happy? Our common approach, which equates happiness with the enjoyment of pleasures, is essentially an attempt to systematically satisfy human desires. The happy life as we conceive it is one where every major wish finds fulfillment—preferably in cinematic fashion—and where suffering is reduced to small discomforts between one emotional peak and the next. The grand, life-encompassing notion of happiness is reduced to a smoothly running mechanism that fulfills what our desires dictate. Desire springs up; desire is satisfied. Pain arises; pain is dealt with. Happiness is obedience to the throne of appetites; unhappiness is a life of wanting and longing and craving.

But are we happy? Hardly, for these two reasons: (1) it is really difficult to attain everything we want; and (2) even if we do, we are not satisfied. We are perpetually driven forward, always waiting for the next enjoyment that will make us feel settled and satisfied. We achieve it, but then we move on to the next pursuit. We are constantly looking for the end of the rainbow, but when it arrives, we don't find the pot of gold. We only find our empty hearts longing for the next promise of fulfillment. In the words of Jean-Jacques Rousseau, we are moved by a "disproportion between our desires and our faculties."[1] Or, as Arthur Schopenhauer added, "Man is never happy, but spends his whole life striving after something he thinks will make him so."[2]

But we do not give up—we try harder. We earn more degrees, start more relationships, accumulate more money, achieve greater professional success, and travel to more exotic locations. But satisfaction of desires does not lead to lasting fulfillment or to a sense of happiness; it is mere satisfaction of desires. It feels as durable as eating cotton candy: "It's sweet for a moment and dissolves an instant later."[3]

This is not a recent insight revealed by psychological studies. Humanity has long suspected that we are not made happy by pursuing, or even achieving, everything we desire. Gregory of Nyssa, for example, described in the fourth century the appetitive nature of our souls: "For as soon as a man satisfies his desire by obtaining what he wants, he starts to desire something else and finds himself empty again; and if he satisfies his desire with this, he becomes empty once again and ready for still another."[4]

Bernard of Clairvaux was another theologian who pinpointed the hopelessness of searching for happiness through the satisfaction of our human appetites: "It is folly and extreme madness always to be longing for things that not only can never satisfy but cannot even blunt the appetite; however much you have of these things, you still desire what you have not yet attained; you are always restlessly sighing after what is missing."[5] Satisfaction of desires is the wrong door to knock on if we expect happiness to be waiting on the other side.

Thinkers across the centuries denounced the bankruptcy of self-centered approaches to happiness. But if we suspect that theologians do not understand much of human nature and would prefer to leave the matter to psychologists, Freud himself arrived at the same conclusion as Gregory and Bernard: "The program of becoming happy, which the pleasure principle imposes on us, cannot be fulfilled. ... By none of the paths [we pursue] can we attain all that we desire."[6]

Or as Jesus put it, "Whoever wants to save their life will lose it."

Jesus already knew of our elusive search for satisfaction. His paradox recognizes at its starting point that our efforts do not take us to the happiness we pursue. The project of trying to satisfy the demands of the self leaves us empty, unsatisfied, and ultimately dead. "To pursue happiness, individually or collectively, as a conscious aim is the surest way to miss it altogether," concluded Malcolm Muggeridge.[7] The program of self-satisfaction does not lead to the ideal of happiness. It's the wrong logic.

What we need is not an improved approach to happiness, or to look for more lasting satisfaction, or to deny the role of desires in life. We do not need an enhanced method, but a total reorientation. Finding happiness is not a matter of searching for it more intently, with greater creativity, or in a more spiritual way. It is a matter of *not searching* for happiness. It is a matter of not living for ourselves but for God and for others.

THE INDIRECTNESS OF HAPPINESS

The search for happiness is elusive because happiness works according to a different dynamic: it is an indirect experience.

We don't find happiness by looking for it because it is not a substance in itself. Instead, happiness finds us—it comes as a *by-product* of a specific orientation to life.

This process is like a young painter longing for artistic greatness.[8] The last thing that will make her great is being obsessed with her own prestige. But she may produce masterpieces if she focuses instead on the properties of light, on the blossoming of flowers, and on the mystical atmosphere the sunrise bestows to lakeside gardens in early spring. True artistic greatness will come as a by-product of other interests that are then depicted in art. It *follows* an artistic orientation.

Or think of someone being interviewed. We will not know him best if he stays focused on himself, watching and restraining every move, calculating words to convey just the right meaning and to present his true self. But we will get a delightful picture of his personality if he lightens up and lets the reporter make him laugh, if he talks passionately about his work, and if he whispers and shouts and pauses, all the while fidgeting with the buttons on his shirt. A person reveals his personality when he is distracted with something else.[9] Others come to know him not when he makes the conscious effort to convey his true self, but when he talks about white chocolate, grocery shopping on Saturday morning, or tucking his daughter into bed.

Happiness also occurs as an indirect affair. A moment will be happier if we forget about it and enjoy the face and the cheesecake in front of us instead of planning for this moment to be happy and measuring it minute by minute on the happiness thermometer. "If only we'd stop trying to be happy, we could have a pretty good time," quipped Edith Wharton.[10]

Happiness is not a result of thinking about happiness, but instead, of being engaged in something else. Paradoxically, we are happy not when we reflect on our happiness, but when we forget about it. Happiness arrives when we let it go. As a psychiatrist has expressed it, "If you observe a really happy man, you will find him building a boat; writing a symphony; educating his son; growing double dahlias in his garden; or looking for dinosaur eggs in the Gobi desert. He will not be searching for happiness as if it were a collar button that has rolled under the radiator."[11]

Happiness is not to be found because it is not an essence but a property; it is not a substance but a possible by-product. Someone does not *possess* happiness. It does not exist in and of itself. It is rather a qualifier—an adjective that characterizes other things. Happiness arrives incidentally, as a consequence. We experience it when we are pursuing something else.

FINDING HAPPINESS BY FORGETTING ABOUT IT

And what is true of moments is true of lifetimes. "Those only are happy ... who make their minds fixed on some object other than their happiness; on the happiness of others, on the improvement of mankind, even on some art or pursuit, followed not as a means, but as itself an ideal end," wrote John Stuart Mill in the nineteenth century. "Aiming thus at something else, they find happiness by the way."[12]

In a paradoxical way, happiness becomes real when we do not make it a direct end. We are used to having other goals be the means to the end of happiness—pursuing things like a challenging job, a welcoming home, and vibrant spirituality for the sake of the fulfillment they will bring. But the paradox of happiness demands that we escape this logic and treat these goals as things to be enjoyed precisely for what they are. Thus, by discovering an interest we can pursue wholeheartedly, we will "incidentally bring happiness in its wake."[13] Self-forgetfulness will permit us to be wholly immersed in an activity or fully attentive in a conversation, so that we lose track of time amidst enjoyment and feel spent, given, and connected.[14]

Viktor Frankl, a neurologist who survived Nazi concentration camps, observed that this indirect nature is a property not only of happiness. For Frankl, the dynamic of consequence can be observed also in other goals we pursue. As a similar phenomenon, Frankl notes that success occurs according to the same logic followed by happiness: as a by-product of focusing and working on things other than success itself. In *Man's Search for Meaning*, he writes,

> For success, like happiness, cannot be pursued; it must ensue, and it only does so as the unintended side-effect of one's personal dedication to a cause greater than oneself or as the by-product of one's surrender to a person other than oneself. … Then you will see that in the long run—in the long run, I say!—success will follow you precisely because you had forgotten to think of it.

In this way, Frankl stresses that success must be forgotten before it can be achieved. It must escape our mental horizon before it can greet us in reality. "Don't aim at success—the more you aim at it and make it a target, the more you are going to miss it. … Happiness must happen, and the same holds for success: you have to let it happen by not caring about it."[15]

An obstacle to this humbler and more realistic enjoyment of life is that we have inflated the notion of happiness. We have pushed aside ideals like God and goodness and love—at least in a pragmatic, unreflective way—and have placed happiness at the throne of human purpose. "In short, the pursuit of happiness has become a distraction, a wrong turning, a mistake. Perhaps it was never the real issue," writes a philosopher.[16] As an ideal, mere contentment cannot sustain the full weight of human dignity, complexity, and splendor. It is not the overarching purpose of life. Happiness is a more modest thing. It is a crowning delight of lives properly lived—an awarded lollipop for the kids who played well.

That's why happiness cannot be found directly. It is not something to be grasped by self-serving efforts because it is a by-product of significant endeavors and relationships.

In the words of Stuart Mill, "The only chance is to treat, not happiness, but some end external to it, as the purpose of life."[17] Individual happiness does not exist for its own sake—as what gives meaning to life. It is a *property* of meaningful lives. And if there isn't meaning or life, there is no happiness. It won't originate itself.

But when we take the momentous step of courage, when we move out of self-centeredness and dare to give up our personal happiness, that's when the great surprise can arrive unannounced. Happiness knocks on our door. It comes to those who are not looking for it. It finds us. When we least expect, when in self-forgetfulness we are engaged in the events of the day and a thrill makes us reflect for a moment, we suddenly notice that life is filled with delights. We feel connected to God and to life; we enjoy an unexpected breeze of joy; we are surprised by a moment of serenity and gratitude. It is an experience of happiness that is not plastic but is humble and authentic—a mature contentment, a reflection of a correct orientation to life. We did not expect it; in fact, happiness felt like an abandoned pursuit. Yet it comes with the freshness of morning. It breathes into our souls; it declares peace and delight upon us; it crowns with joy an ordinary day when we forgot about our well-being and simply *lived*.

THE GIFT OF HAPPINESS

And here lies the paradox of happiness. The aim of our existence can be attained if it ceases to be our aim. We can find happiness if we stop searching for it. In Jesus' words, we have life when abundant life is not our objective. We achieve by giving up; we find by looking elsewhere. Contentment comes as an unexpected visitor, knocking on hearts concerned about things other than themselves. As an ancient saying expresses, "Happiness is the absence of the striving for happiness."[18] Efforts to earn and attain are to be replaced by receptivity, by serenely waiting for this dessert of life.[19] Or as Nathaniel Hawthorne has put it, "Happiness is a butterfly, which, when pursued, is always beyond our grasp, but which, if you sit down quietly, may alight upon you."[20]

Happiness escapes the bent-in logic we live by, as does every good gift God gave us. Satisfaction is not a matter of putting the self in the center of our existence, as sin has taught us. To start with the self is to end with nothing but the self. But when we enter the rhythm of life, the logic of the universe; when we step out of the selfish posture of sin and step into the dance of love, self-giving, and joy at the heart of reality; when we dare to live not for our own sake, but for others, like God does; when we look at life as a wondrous gift of grace that comes undeserved and unannounced, waiting to be received in humility; when we live as the loving creatures we were made to be, that's when happiness can arrive as God's gift to crown our holy living with delight.

And if happiness arrives as a gift, in another great paradox, it can only be kept if it is given back to others. Only by releasing do we hold on to it. "Happiness can only be complete when it is given to others," describes James Houston. "We simply cannot hold on to happiness. We have to give it away before we, and others, can truly enjoy it."[21] This means that the best way to keep a moment of joy is to share it with someone else. A lonely dive into the sea can be fun for a few minutes, but it can be a milestone of celebration if we call friends and spend hours telling jokes, floating around, remembering childhood beach trips, and talking about fears and dreams and nonsense.

Shared happiness is extended happiness. We will enlarge our joy when we enter its freely received, freely given dance. As Ralph Sockman describes, "Love, sympathy, appreciation do not exhaust themselves by use. They are saved by being spent. ... Human nature cannot be locked up for safe-keeping. It can be saved only by spending."[22] If joy arrives to us freely, it will remain on its journey when it is freely distributed. An open hand cannot hold on to things, but it is the only way of receiving more. A closed fist neither receives nor keeps; it can only crush.

How can we live, then, in a way that happiness can surprise us? Which attitudes of life exclude happiness, and which ones invite it in? How does the dynamic of forgetting about happiness and sharing it with others work? Happiness arrives, as we will see, to those who learn to live beyond the rule of the self.

CHAPTER 5
Beyond the Rule of the Self

A young man opened the window of his room to admire the landscape. It was an autumn night in 1889. He painted his view over Saint-Rémy, France, portraying a picturesque village lit by a sky ablaze with the moon and stars, flowing with waves of light—a living heaven of movement and color. A bush ascending like flames united the quiet village with the fecundity of life above, as a connector between houses, streets, and the vivid surroundings that witnessed its sleep. "This morning I saw the country from my window a long time before sunrise, with nothing but the morning star, which looked very big," he recorded later, almost like a reminder of a memory now superseded by its vivid artistic representation.[1]

Vincent van Gogh's post-impressionist style was experimenting with a new perspective on art. Similar to the works of friends like Gauguin and Cézanne, Van Gogh set out to portray his own inner, subjective experience of the sights before him rather than the fixed objects of the scene. "He painted his own artistic, poetic, emotional reactions, his visions," explains H. R. Rookmaaker.[2] Considered by many to be Van Gogh's magnum opus, *The Starry Night* convenes an impression, an intuition, a reaction. It is a scene from a point of view. It is the amalgam of feeling of an artist inviting us to his own experience of reality.

The Starry Night and other post-impressionist paintings are a visual representation of subjectivity. Van Gogh illustrates with canvas and brushstrokes that we do not approach scenes passively, with no interest or perspective. Rather, we *invest* something of ourselves into everything we experience. We concede meaning and feeling to the situations before our eyes. We join them, so to speak, with our unique state of spirit. We give of ourselves, sprinkle reality with our hearts, and project our souls into events and people around us. As beings who experience the world, we communicate of ourselves by the very act of living.

SELFLESS HAPPINESS

Happiness, in this same logic, is a product of selflessness. It is a consequence of engagement, of surrender, of participation. It requires an attentive and interested posture to the world. It is like God's dew for those who look outward. Curved people cannot get it—they are not open to it.

But how does happiness grow out of selflessness? How does this dynamic take shape in practice? Let's explore the posture of life that conducts to the surprise of happiness and observe, in contrast, the ways in which our self-centeredness excludes the possibility of happiness. A comparison between selfishness—curved and closed in on itself—and selflessness—open to life—illuminates how selflessness is the posture that realizes the indirect dynamic of happiness.

If we pause to observe for a moment, who are the happiest people you know? Probably, they will also be some of the most selfless people around you. And who are the least happy? The most self-centered. Selfless people are free to see things that will not necessarily benefit them. They are not driven by self-interest and thus can be interested in others for their own sake. They are not caged within their selfishness; they are free to wander and roam and encounter. For instance, when they meet someone, they are not compelled to use the other person for individual attention or for benefit; they can simply appreciate that person. A psychologist examined this process, explaining that self-interest "fosters self-absorption and thereby constricts the range and depth of gratifications available in pursuing interests in other people, activities, and events."[3] In other words, selfishness closes us within ourselves, but self-forgetfulness opens us up to the splendor around us.

Self-centeredness is like a bubble that severs us from reality. It dims our power of attention and disperses our ability to get interested, like a drunken absorption in ourselves that sees people and events around us as vague figures. In the words of Matt Jenson, "The narrowness of such a gaze, caused by its attention to only one object, causes us to miss the world (not to mention God) for what it is. All else sits in fuzziness of peripheral vision and is only seen in reference to the primary object, ourselves."[4] Such self-focused vision also gives us glasses of self-interest that can primarily differentiate between two colors: what benefits me, and what doesn't. This binary vision impoverishes our minds. We don't really look at things; we glimpse others through ourselves.

Selflessness, on the other hand, can look around—it can *connect* with reality. We start to notice things around us and become fascinated with the colors, textures, and melodies we find. It's like someone who just moved up to the ground level. The basement of self-centeredness was stuffy and colorless, uncreative and tedious. But now, in an expansive, self-forgetful posture to life, there is light; there is warmth; there are windows; there are neighbors; there are parties. There is a whole world to interact with—beauty and intelligence beyond ourselves. Normal routine turns into a feast for the senses; other people become continents to be explored. Relationships ascend to a whole new level: We start to listen, to appreciate, to love. We learn to notice the charming pleasures hidden in a fellow human being.

Such a self-forgetful attitude allows us to open up and savor the banquet flourishing all around us, if only we have eyes to see. "Where, then, does happiness lie? In forgetfulness, not indulgence, of the self," observes Malcolm Muggeridge. "We live in a dark, self-enclosed prison which is all we see or know if our glance is fixed ever downwards. To lift it upwards, becoming aware of the wide, luminous universe outside—this alone is happiness." Our self-enclosed prison prevents from *seeing*—if not in a physical sense, certainly with existential and spiritual eyes. So Muggeridge continues on to describe the diverse and abundant pleasures uncovered by a selfless, outward-facing posture to life: "Human love; the delights and beauties of our dear earth, its colors and shapes and sounds; the enchantment of understanding and laughing, and all other exercise of such faculties we possess; the marvel of the meaning of everything, fitfully glimpsed, inadequately expounded, but ever-present."[5]

Sadly, most people are imprisoned within their own egos. They can look outward only when and how the ego lets them. They must live under the unbendable rules of self-satisfaction. They hardly play, hardly waste, hardly rest; they live to serve their egos. They are not free, as the pursuit of every desire promises. They are imprisoned, for they *rarely do anything other than what their desires dictate*. And you quickly learn that desires are a fairly uncreative bunch. Satisfying them all will bore and enslave us to death.

But freedom from the rule of self enables us to live for a higher purpose. We can transcend the colorless likeness selfishness imprints on us all: everyone looking for success, comfort, security, prestige—one uncreative parade of sameness. How different and interesting are those who live for things higher than themselves, who make their days one stirring offering before God and some great cause in the world, and who bathe their existence with significance beyond their own personal happiness. A higher purpose consumes and stretches us. It makes us grow beyond our years and enlivens us with passion and interest. It transforms the scope of our days from survival to mission. It replaces the lenses of the self before our eyes with a God-infused view of all things.

OPENING UP TO LIFE

How is it that opening up to life affects our experience of happiness? In this way: Selfless living will achieve precisely what self-centeredness was looking for all along. The pleasure mortified by those obsessed with it will now grace people who do not live for pleasure and so are surprised by moments filled with life. They enjoy a broadening of the self, a wideness of experience. They are able to savor a larger breadth of existence. Their range of emotions grows to include compassion, transcendence, love, vigor, benevolence, child-like awe—and happiness, surprisingly and delightfully, like a sunset breeze. The self that was previously curved within itself expands outward, having learned to embrace and thus to stretch itself wide.

Self-centeredness, in contrast, tries to expand by appropriating and absorbing everything as its own. C. S. Lewis points out that our famine of spirit drives us to make another person's "intellectual and emotional life just an extension of ours, make him hate our hatreds, resent our quarrels, and give way to our own selfishness through him, just as through ourselves."[6] Selfishness seeks to conquer until every inch of reality is called "mine." It will charm and snob and exploit until starvation and isolation are all that's left—until, ironically, nothing can be called "mine," not even itself.

Selflessness does expand our souls, but by an alternative logic: by rejoicing and living in others. People become part of our life not because we absorb their thoughts and will into ours, but because we join their lives as fellow creatures. We do not need personal victories in order to rejoice, since we can celebrate just as well a friend's success. We can observe people in the park and laugh for joy. Selfless people can live for others and thus live *in* others, and thus live *beyond* themselves.

We have mastered the art of selfishness, but only as a twisted logic sin has taught us. We have been bent in, but that's not our original nature. Under the curving weight of sin is a marvelous creation after God's own image and likeness. In our deepest impulses and reflexes, beneath the cauldron of craving and restlessness, we desire to function as God does. Our souls aspire to invite, feast, and laugh—to connect, help, and serve. They long to expand, include, and contribute. We were not made to be grumpy, closed sheds, but expansive beacons of love.

Nothing could be more logical, therefore, than happiness being the crowning outcome of a *good* life—of days lived with love and the passion that comes from holiness, kindness, peace, and wonder. For happiness is a property of true life. It is not a product of chance, nor is it divorced from the ethical texture of existence. Rather, it is an aspect of life lived the way God is— full of selflessness and love for others. It is the surprise awaiting those who have an outward orientation, who have forgotten about their own happiness and lived for God, for others, and for the gospel. What we try to get is grasped instead when we give.

AN INVITATION TO SELFLESSNESS

The conclusion is that if we are to experience happiness—to give it up as our supreme goal in life, forget about ourselves and live for God and others—we have to step out of self-centeredness as much as we can. Maybe we can't fully overcome the curved logic of sin, but we can accept the challenge of an open and generous life. "If man were truly happy it would be in unconscious self-forgetfulness that his greatest happiness would lie, like the saints and God,"[7] affirmed Blaise Pascal.

The task now at hand, therefore, and the theme of the following chapters, is to remove the ego as the ruler of our lives. It is, in the words of Jesus, to lay down our lives for him and the gospel. Let's explore how Jesus invites us to lose our lives so we can gain life—with his intriguing call to deny ourselves and follow him: "Whoever wants to be my disciple must deny themselves and take up their cross and follow me" (Mark 8:34).

The key to the paradox of happiness lies just before the paradox. Jesus' invitation may sound radical, but if we gain life when we lay down our lives, wouldn't the call to fullness of life also be paradoxical? Jesus points to his own path leading to the cross and invites us to join him in the paradoxical shape of life glittering at the heart of reality.

PART THREE

The Rhythm of the Liberated Life

CHAPTER 6
Opening Up to Life

It was one of the happiest moments I'd experienced in a long time. Happier than the lazy Saturday at home, watching TV all day and killing every hint of hunger with chips, chocolate, and ice cream. Happier than the day I spent in a bookstore savoring book after book, changing from one to the next according to the wishes of the moment. Happier than the holiday cruise, with its numerous meals, paradisiacal beaches, and the bubbling Jacuzzi to relax in while watching the sunset.

This day was quite different: a marathon of preaching sermons in three church services and interacting with people all day long. It was exhausting, a day without many comforts. But my heart overflowed with happiness.

The message was about the life of Simon the fisherman, who became Peter the rock. I narrated episodes of Peter's life with Jesus—the net full of fish when Jesus called Peter to be a fisher of men, the day when Peter dared to walk on water with Jesus, the final dinner in which Jesus shared bread and wine. Then there was the moment that would define the course of Peter's life: the night when he denied Jesus three times around a charcoal fire. In the crucial test, the rock crumbled, and Peter revealed himself to be just the old Simon. When Jesus had talked about the cross and self-denial, Peter was all in. Now that the cross had arrived, Peter did not deny himself and follow Jesus, but denied Jesus and followed his own way, weeping bitterly.

A few weeks later, Jesus met Peter on a beach. Incorporating elements of many of their encounters—filling another fishing net, like the net of the day of Peter's call; making Peter swim against the waves to the beach; breaking bread around a fire—Jesus made Peter arrive consciously to another crucial moment: to be asked three times around a charcoal fire whether he loved Jesus. And this time, Peter passed the test. From now on, his future wouldn't be defined by his triple denial of Jesus around a fire, but by his triple affirmation of Jesus around a fire. Jesus offered Peter a new memory to redirect his life. From then on, the rock would stay firm.

Peter's story touched people's hearts. Many tears fell as we heard Jesus offering Peter a new past, a new mission, and a new life. People came forward to pray and throw pieces of paper into the fire that burned during the service—notes describing a memory they wanted to redeem. A man came to tell me that on that day he understood that something in his past was holding him back, and that he now felt free. An old lady came to hug me but did not say a word. Another man came weeping and told me he was a former pastor who had been disqualified for ministry by a sin two years before. He raised his eyes—which had been staring down until that moment—looked me in the eyes, and said, "Look at me. I talk to you like I would talk to Jesus." His next sentence will remain in my memory forever: "I'm back!"

Meeting those people brought a well-being to my soul unlike anything else. Their eyes shone with new opportunity. If Jesus had redeemed Peter's past, they too could be free from the prison of the past. It's hard to imagine the traumas described in the notes burnt in the fire. Possibly memories of betrayals, disappointments, and fractured relationships were consumed there.

I was exploding with happiness. It had been a tiring day, but my heart beamed with the opportunity—a brief island of service in my sea of selfishness and self-absorption—to forget myself for some moments, serve God, and see people being changed. It was a day to deny my preoccupation with myself and to focus on God and others. But above all, it was a day to witness another process of denial and affirmation: after denying Jesus, Peter had a chance to affirm him. This encounter changed the course of his life.

We explored Jesus' paradox in Mark 8:35—"For whoever wants to save their life will lose it, but whoever loses their life for me and for the gospel will save it"—in Part Two. In the next chapters, let's explore *how* we can lose our life and live for Jesus, and thus gain it. What do we do to live Jesus' paradox of happiness?

Jesus gives us this *how* in the preceding verse: "Whoever wants to be my disciple must deny themselves and take up their cross and follow me" (Mark 8:34).[1] Self-denial, taking up one's cross, and following Jesus is what one does to lose one's life for Jesus and the gospel, and thus to save it. Jesus' invitation to discipleship is the key to selflessness, and so it is the key to happiness.

Let's start with the first of Jesus' three descriptions of what it means to be a disciple—to deny oneself—and explore the other two in the following chapters.

JESUS' CALL TO SELF-DENIAL

Self-denial has traditionally been understood in negative terms, unfortunately. It is often equated with repression of oneself and associated with cynicism, gloom, and negativity; with lack of self-esteem and disregard of one's well-being; with rejection of human joy and human desires. It is a virtue that, at best, people admire but wouldn't want for themselves. The common picture of self-denial is that of a cranky old man who is earnest but lifeless—someone whose biggest concern is to find people enjoying themselves.

Self-denial has gained the stereotype of being the denial of fun. This notion has emerged because, traditionally, self-denial has been identified with just one of its many facets: asceticism. So, self-denial became a matter of bodily rigors, deprivation of food and sleep, introspection and isolation, extreme concern with sin, and extreme rejection of sexuality. It came to be linked with self-imposed suffering, lack of enjoyment of life, and repression of desires. But asceticism is only a part of what Jesus means by denying oneself, and if we focus on just this ascetic aspect—and on its most extreme examples—we will miss the purpose of Jesus' call altogether. The spiritual practices designed for aiding self-denial are not what self-denial consists of, nor are they ends in themselves.[2] They are just means to a grander reorientation of the self.

To understand this better, we can imagine a man striving after fortune who endures toil and hardships to reach his million-dollar goal. The desire for wealth consumes him to the point that everything else becomes subordinated to it. He wakes up early in the morning and denies himself the pleasure of sleeping in. He works around the clock and denies himself time with family. He pours his income into investments and denies himself the satisfaction of basic needs. He seeks the company of wealthy people and avoids friendships that hold no financial advantage. He works to the point of exhaustion and undertakes sacrifices worthy of missionaries in the most demanding fields and of monks in the strictest monasteries.

But we ask, has he denied himself? Of course not. On the contrary, he yielded to his own self. He let his ego rule and distort his life. The hardships he endured were not self-denial; they were expressions of self-centeredness. He undertook sacrifices, certainly, but for his own sake.

Self-denial is often thought of as denial of the self as *subject*—as the fountain of human action. This perspective makes self-denial a matter of weakening the impulses of the self. It tries to repress desires and mortify the strength of our hearts, as if a weaker self would be a holier self. The final hope is to have a domesticated "I," where vigilance and spiritual exercises suppress, if not extinguish, every human impulse with some element of sin in it.

But denial of the self as subject is impossible—and theologically misguided. The self will always be the subject of our lives; it will always be the "I" from which we live. We have no other. To get rid of the self is to get rid of ourselves: it is to cease to be persons, and that's impossible. Moreover, this approach is theologically misguided because it confuses sanctification with repression. *God* gave us selves. They are marred by sin, and we have to resist sinful desires, yet our selves were created by God to be the subject of our lives. As God's creation, they have eternal value. They are images of God's own self.

The essence of self-denial is denial of the self not as subject, but as *object* of our lives. It is denial of the self as the reigning purpose of human action, as the master we live to please, as the god for which we exist. It is denial of the logic of life centered on the self and converging to it.

That's why our friend striving after fortune did not deny himself. He ignored and repressed his self as the *subject* in order to subordinate other impulses to the ambition of becoming rich. But his self was the looming *object* of his pursuit. He was living for no other aim than to please himself. He was his god; he was his master; he was his own purpose. Though he went through hardships, his sacrifices were expressions of self-centeredness. He let his self exert such gravity as an object that it engulfed the "I" from which he lived. He battered his self, ironically, out of self-interest. We can see the foolishness of it all.

We have seen how sin turns us inward, and how it twists and curves our souls into ourselves. Self-denial is the gradual attitude by which we begin the untwisting, the opening outward. It is a steady reorientation of the self, a redirection of the logic under which we function. The inward movement of self-centeredness—attracting all our thoughts, perceptions, emotions, and actions to the service and exaltation of the self— starts a magnificent reversal. We disallow the self as the converging purpose of our lives. Its gravitational power starts to weaken. The misty atmosphere of self-centeredness dissipates to reveal a luminous, beautiful universe.

Self-denial is the attitude that gradually purifies our purpose in life. It purges our logic of functioning until we see and value the self for what it is: a marvelous creation of God, but not the center of reality. Self-denial offers a mature perspective, where the self is no longer what we live for (though we still live by it), and where the self is no longer the lens we see through, coloring people and circumstances in accordance with possible advantages that may be gained. Self-denial is the process by which we remove the self as our chief love—loving others as they aid the love of the self—to start to direct our beings toward a new center: God. Then we can start, in the terms Jesus used, to love God above everything, love others as ourselves, and love ourselves appropriately. We deny life for our own sake and focus on other ends for which to exist: God, above all, and the flourishing of everything in him. Our self is to be just our self: not the whole of reality, but a delightful agent for love and redemption in the world.

SELF-DENIAL AS PROPER EXPRESSION OF THE SELF

This means that the purpose of self-denial is not repression, but rather correct expression of the self. The goal is not a weak, battered being, but someone turned outward in holy strength. We do repress sinful impulses, but it is not repression for repression's sake. Repression is just a first step toward a grander rechanneling designed to remove the focus from ourselves and to "turn the man's attention away from self to [God], and to the man's neighbors."[3] For example, self-denial for someone struggling with sexual temptation is not repression of himself into an asexual being, but it is correct expression of his desire for intimacy toward God, his sexuality toward his spouse, and his craving for connection toward and in service of others. Self-denial for someone yielding to gluttony is not repression of hunger to the point of starvation, but it is correct expression of hunger for healthy food and proper enjoyment of it. Self-denial for someone desiring glory for himself is not the rejection of the concept of glory, but rather the correct expression of working for God's glory in everything he does. Self-denial does not consist in repression and weakening and mortification per se. Its final purpose is a reorientation of the self. As John Stott puts it, "True self-denial (the denial of our false, fallen self) is not the road to self-destruction but the road to self-discovery."[4] It is the attitude that straightens our bent souls away from ourselves and toward God and people around us.[5]

This process is neither easy nor immediate. It is gradual—a counterintuitive posture we cultivate every day. It involves discomfort similar to the practice of physiotherapy: only bit by bit are we able to move an arm that was previously immobile. But we know that each milestone along the way—the ability to hold a cup of water, to stretch out our arms to hug someone—makes the effort worthwhile. All the more so with the soul: it begins to embrace the healthy functioning of someone not distorted by egotism but made mature in his understanding of himself and made loving in his relationships to God and others.

This dynamic includes an accurate assessment of the positive role of human desires. Someone who truly practices self-denial is not the gloomy person we have described, but a radiant, lively person who is deeply satisfied. She is someone who has risen above herself and is now enjoying life to the fullest. And the satisfactions of self-centeredness pale in comparison. As C. S. Lewis puts it,

> We are half-hearted creatures, fooling about with drink and sex and ambition when infinite joy is offered us, like an ignorant child who wants to go on making mud pies in a slum because he cannot imagine what is meant by the offer of a holiday at the sea. We are far too easily pleased.[6]

The problem is not desires per se, like in the Stoic and Buddhist perspectives, as if desires were something bad. No, they are a wonderful gift from God to propel us outward and to make us interested in the reality around us. It is difficult to imagine how even more self-absorbed we would be were it not for these impulses that attract us to things and people other than ourselves.

The question is rather what our desires are directed *to*. The process of sanctification is not one of repression but of reorientation of desires. When we learn to express ourselves properly, redirect our lives for the thrill of living rightly, and enjoy

God and others, we are, now unsurprisingly, happy. We obey the nature of desiring; we are propelled outward. We engage with life around us, and happiness can arrive as a by-product.

SELF-DENIAL IS THE DOOR
TO PROPER LOVE OF SELF

Self-denial is an ugly-sounding word, but it names the attitude by which we come to live rightly, healthily, and happily. It is an opening outward, an exit from the suffocating prison of self-centeredness. It is denial of the idol of the self—which stifles everything under its craving and distorts lives who seek to function as if they were a god—to embrace a healthy self who lives true to itself and is thus mature and well. If happiness can arrive as a by-product of being self-forgetfully immersed in life, self-denial is the daily process to turn us away from ourselves. It is the embrace of the beautiful creatures we were meant to be and of the thrill of living under God.

The main effect of such a proper view of the self, among uncounted others, is that we learn to love in the truest sense. When we love a thing for the sake of something else, we may actually love the benefit sought after, not what embodies or delivers it.[7] When we come to love people for reasons other than our own benefit, we start to indeed love them. All else may have been, underneath it all, self-love. Instead of loving others as ourselves, we loved ourselves in our love of others. We loved others because, at its core, it was a love of ourselves.

This does not mean that self-love is essentially harmful. On the contrary, self-love is good and holy because it is love of something valuable created by God.[8] The problem occurs when self-love is so central to us that it prevents us from loving others, or when it collapses the love of others under the love of the self. It becomes our functional god and distorts our relationships with everything else. But when God is the foundation of our existence and the basis for our loving, and when we love the self for God's sake, self-love can be proper and valid. We come to value the self not as the absolute reality we live for, but as a worthy creature designed by God. Self-love is valid when its gravitational logic is reversed: when it is part of our love of God. To love God is not to disdain other things, but to love God firstly and everything else in him.

Thus self-denial, in another paradox, produces mature self-love. "Wholesome self-love is to love God more than self," writes Bernard of Clairvaux, explaining that self-love that is true to itself—that seeks the highest good possible to the self—seeks what is most rewarding, and so loves God above oneself. It is love that acknowledges that there is nothing more delightful to us than to savor God's presence. "He alone knows how to love himself who loves God," he writes. "Self-love can do no more than seek earnestly to enjoy the supreme and true Good."[9] When we grasp the extent of pleasures that self-denial grants us—adoration, benevolence, serenity, hope—we see that it is the attitude most advantageous to us.

When the incurvature of the self gradually straightens up, we learn to love God, love others, and even love ourselves properly. We can appreciate people for who they are, without the need to absorb them into our self-relation. And we can also appreciate ourselves for who we are, free from the inclination to bow to the self as if it were a god. Free from the rule of the self, we grow mature, healthy, and happy.

SURRENDERING THE SELF

Yet we must not forget that self-denial consists in *denial*, nor should we hope to seek it lightly. "For we who are alive are always being given over to death for Jesus' sake," wrote Paul, "so that his life may also be revealed in our mortal body" (2 Cor 4:11). Similarly, Dietrich Bonhoeffer expressed the process of denying the god of the self with firm words: "When Christ calls a man, he bids him come and die."[10] We will not be able to taste the pleasures of selflessness while we are still interested in those pleasures selfishly, nor will we exercise self-denial as long as happiness is still our aim and self-service is our standard mode of operating. Only a self given to Christ will be a new self, as C. S. Lewis expressed:

> Christ says: "Give me All. I don't want so much of your time and so much of your money and so much of your work: I want You. I have not come to torment your natural self, but to kill it. No half-measures are any good. I don't want to cut a branch here and a branch there, I want to have the whole tree down. Hand over the whole natural self, all the desires which you think innocent as well as the ones you think wicked—the whole outfit. I will give you a new self instead. In fact, I will give you Myself: my own shall become yours." ... Look for yourself, and you will find in the long run only hatred, loneliness, despair, rage, ruin, and decay. But look to Christ and you will find Him, and with Him everything else thrown in.[11]

To practice self-denial and taste its delights, we strive to dethrone the self as the ultimate end of our lives. We try to gradually remove self-absorption from our thoughts and to soak our minds with the majesty of God. The more our love for God grows, the easier and tastier will be our love for others, and the healthier our love for ourselves. We strive to let our preoccupation with ourselves go, and in the moments when we are able to do it—when we are immersed in gratitude and adoration of God, enjoying the beauty of his presence and the sweetness of relationships and the delights of God's creation—suddenly we notice how glad we feel. Paradoxically, we lose our lives to gain life and live to the full.

Only what is lost can be saved. Only what is dead can be resurrected. Only a forgotten happiness can arrive as a surprise.

CHAPTER 7
Getting by Giving

Around AD 362, at some fancy palace dressed in marble, Emperor Julian was fuming. The last of Rome's pagan emperors was leading a final effort to revive the religious practices that were withering under a world turning Christian. Devotion to Caesar and to the pantheon gods was being replaced by devotion to a rebel who had been crucified a few centuries back in an obscure corner of the empire. How dare they?

One of Julian's focuses was the building of charities, reasoning that moral character was the secret behind Christian growth. Indeed, when calamitous plagues decimated millions of people throughout the Roman Empire, it was the Christians who headed relief efforts to care for the sick in a context that virtually lacked social services. Thus, Julian complained that, "when the poor happened to be neglected and overlooked by the [pagan] priests, the impious Galileans observed this and devoted themselves to benevolence." In Julian's eyes, their shrewdness was so great that they even "support[ed] not only their poor, but ours as well, everyone can see that our people lack aid from us."[1]

Julian's efforts failed. It is not simple, after all, to summon multitudes of people to start caring for strangers who are sick and dying—especially when the disease was infectious and many who cared for the moribund ended up switching places with them, dying in their stead, while the sick regained health and came back to life. As historian Rodney Stark concludes, Julian's mission failed because it lacked a core belief: "Paganism had failed to develop the kind of voluntary system of good works that Christians had been constructing for more than three centuries; moreover, paganism lacked the religious ideas that would have made such organized efforts plausible."[2] Julian's state-enforced organization lacked the reasoning needed to mobilize people for costly self-giving. Why should someone care for a stranger while the world was collapsing under a plague and one could become a victim of his care of others?

The humble folks from Galilee had a motivation no one else had. Those simple peasants, artisans, widows, and slaves had received a moral injection that transformed their outlook on life: their God had died in their stead. He had accepted wounds that were not his own. He had died so that they could live. They were survivors of a trade-off—people with a story to tell and a sacrifice to emulate. Love of strangers was costly, but someone had already given himself for them. They had been saved by a cross, and they now imitated the self-giving of their Master.

When Jesus explains what it means to follow him toward the cross in Mark 8:34, he invites us first to an abstaining activity: denial of the self we live for. Then he calls us to an active movement: he invites us to take up our crosses.

THE CROSS JESUS TOOK UP

The key detail to notice here is that Jesus had just solemnly revealed his own destiny, which was marked by the cross: "He then began to teach them that the Son of Man must suffer many things and be rejected by the elders, the chief priests and the teachers of the law, and that he must be killed and after

three days rise again" (Mark 8:31). The announcement of Jesus'
impending death is what prompted this radical call to discipleship. Jesus starts his journey to Jerusalem and the death that
awaits him there, so he invites his followers to walk the same
cruciform path.

The invitation to take up one's cross, therefore, is thor-
oughly shaped by the cross Jesus took up. We need not spec-
ulate what taking up our crosses might possibly mean; Jesus
established the model for us. He has invited us to follow him,
so the crosses we take up are patterned after the one our Master
took up.[3]

We could fill a library with books discussing the meaning
of Jesus' cross. But our subject here is not so much what his
cross accomplished (such as expiation of sins and victory over
evil), but rather what it expressed of Jesus' own person. If we
are to take up our crosses, our question is: What did it mean *for
Jesus* to take up his cross? What is the pattern that Jesus' cross
established for us to follow?

The central passage in the New Testament for understanding Jesus' attitude toward his life and death is Philippians 2:5–8:

> In your relationships with one another, have the same
> mindset as Christ Jesus: Who, being in very nature God,
> did not consider equality with God something to be
> used to his own advantage; rather, he made himself
> nothing by taking the very nature of a servant, being
> made in human likeness. And being found in appear-
> ance as a man, he humbled himself by becoming obe-
> dient to death—even death on a cross!

This passage calls us to have the same attitude Jesus had—
not considering who he was for his own advantage. Jesus did
not live his life in the Godhead, as well as his life on earth, for

his own sake, for the service of his self. His divine nature and equality with God were not things he lived *for*; they were just the being he lived *from*. His life was a constant offering of obedience before the Father and of service to people around him. Jesus was not centered on himself; we do not see Jesus preoccupied with his comfort, success, or glory. Rather, his mind was focused on fulfilling his destiny and displaying the glory of the Father.

If seeking advantage was what Jesus did not do, Philippians 2:7 describes what he lived for: he took the "nature of a servant." He denied his own self—"made himself nothing"[4]—in order to live as a servant, as one who gives of himself. Jesus let go his privileges as a divine person to live within the limitations of a human being "made in human likeness." This movement represented an emptying of his self and a posture of self-giving. He became one defined by his *service*.

This twofold movement of self-denial and self-giving—of living not for his own advantage but to serve others—Jesus obeyed to death on a cross. The cross was the climax of Jesus' attitude: there he denied himself most fully and gave of himself most visibly. The cross Jesus took up was his grand display of love, the giving-away of his very self. His cruciform act is one of self-denial and self-giving.

CRUCIFORM LIFE

That's the pattern we follow when Jesus calls us to take up our cross. Jesus illustrated the alternative logic of life we are being invited to: he was not self-centered, but lived for others' sake. He reversed the movement of seeking one's own advantage to assume the nature of a servant. "Christ's death [was] his act of love, specifically his act of renouncing status, and thus refraining from any act of selfishness or self-interest, for the benefit of others," summarizes Michael Gorman. Christ is thus "the embodiment of status-renouncing, self-giving, others-oriented love."[5] That was the logic by which Jesus functioned. His dominant attitude in life, his model on the cross, and thus the pattern for our own crosses, is service of others instead of self-service, self-giving in the place of self-assertion. That's what it means to take up our cross as he took his. We are to give of ourselves and love others as Christ did.

It is worth clarifying that there is a tradition of interpretation that understands Jesus' invitation to take up our cross differently. It is a tradition that identifies Jesus' invitation to take up one's cross primarily with suffering—a tradition that is venerable, but I believe misguided. John Calvin, for example, connects the cross of Jesus' followers to "a hard, laborious, troubled life, a life full of many and various kinds of evils."[6] In a similar way, classic commentator Matthew Henry equates our crosses with suffering: "The cross is here put for all sufferings, as men or Christians; providential afflictions, persecutions for righteousness' sake, every trouble that befalls us, either for doing well or for not doing ill."[7]

I grant, of course, that Jesus' cross contained tremendous suffering, and that living in obedience and self-giving also results in many hardships. But Jesus did not live and did not ascend to the cross for *suffering's sake*. The primary purpose of his cross was, instead, redemption. Suffering was included, but it was not what Jesus died for. It was a means, not an end. In the words of G. K. Chesterton, Jesus' death was not the death of the suicide, who dies for the sake of dying, but that of the hero, who dies for the sake of living.[8]

Taking up our crosses, therefore, is not to be equated with the sufferings we undergo (though suffering is certainly part of it), but with Jesus' pattern of self-denial and self-giving. "The cross Jesus invites his hearers to take up refers not to the burdens life imposes from without but rather to painful, redemptive action voluntarily undertaken for others," explains a commentator.[9] We should not glorify suffering—in Jesus' cross or in our own—as if suffering were something good in itself. We should not desire it, as Christ did not when he prayed in the garden at Gethsemane. But we should be ready to accept the hardships included in following Jesus' example of living for God and others. We welcome suffering not for its own sake, but for the sake of giving of ourselves as Jesus did.

That's the reversal movement Martin Luther hinted at in his definition of sin as being curved in on oneself. If sin turned us inward and made us self-centered, holiness implies turning outward and being oriented toward others. Luther expressed this ideal as "a man [who] does not live for himself alone in this mortal body to work for it alone, but [who] lives also for all men on earth."[10] Sanctification brings a fundamental reorientation of ourselves. Sin turned us inward, but Jesus stretches us wide as a loving, cruciform embrace of the world.

To take up one's cross means to join Jesus in his generous logic of life, his marvelous mission of redeeming humanity. It consists in taking the nature of a servant to live for God and for those around us. It involves removing the self as the center around which our lives, thoughts, and actions circle, and through the practice of self-denial making it only the fountain out of which our love and service flow. To take up one's cross is to have self-giving as our primary posture in life.

A SELF-GIVING GOD

The foundations for such a life posture run deeper still, for Jesus' cross was not an isolated incident. It was the acting out in history of God's own self-giving nature. It is not an "arbitrary expression of the nature of God," according to Rowan Williams, but "what the life of the Trinity is, translated into the world."[11] The cross is the consequence of the encounter between rebellious humanity and the loving community of Father, Son, and Spirit, that opens itself to embrace and redeem the world in Jesus' outstretched arms. "When God sets out to embrace the enemy, the result is the cross," writes Miroslav Volf. "On the cross the dancing circle of self-giving and mutually indwelling divine persons opens up for the enemy; in the agony of the passion the movement stops for a brief moment and a fissure appears so that sinful humanity can join in."[12] Such fissure—such grand entrance—is God's invitation to the festive fellowship Father, Son, and Spirit enjoy. In the cross God extends humanity his hand, so to speak, to invite us to his eternal, shared life. In the words of Dallas Willard, "The aim of God in history is the creation of an all-inclusive community of loving persons with God himself at the very heart of this community as its prime Sustainer and most glorious Inhabitant."[13]

Even before creating the world, God was inherently relational. As a triune community of Father, Son, and Spirit, there is intrinsic relatedness in the divine nature. Such shared life is like a divine dance twirling from eternity to eternity: a community of divine persons who move in each other and offer space for the movement of the others; a dance of self-surrender and self-giving; a mutual interweaving and indwelling of divine persons in one another. "Each Person receives everything from the others and at the same time gives everything to the others," points out another theologian.[14] As a community of persons, God is fundamentally relational. Self-giving is the basic posture of God's nature.

This affects the way we understand reality and what it means to be human. If the Creator of the universe is a community of persons, then "being means communion."[15] A person is not a self-enclosed substance but is constituted by his relationships to God and others. To be a person implies a "movement towards communion which leads to a transcendence of the boundaries of the 'self' "; it means "a movement of mutual love among us in the out-going and responding of persons to one another."[16] This is the reason why being curved in on oneself is such a disorder of personhood: being a person is something inherently relational. To be self-centered is to shy away from the fundamental dynamic of existence and to evade the community of love God is gathering in himself. Self-centeredness enfolds us in ourselves, but selflessness grants the opening posture needed for relationships, love, and communion. Because God is a triune community of persons, a human being functions in the image of God when she nurtures a self-giving posture that generates loving relationships.

The cross is the great reversal of history—God's abrupt interruption to install the reign of love. The moment that liberates the world, the pinnacle of the drama of redemption, the resolution for the accumulated sins and conflicts and cruelty of millennia, is the moment when God gave himself for his creatures. God reversed the tide of self-centeredness with an epicenter of self-giving.

BREATHING GRACE EVERYWHERE

This act of love shook everything and sent waves that shaped all that exists. Self-giving is imprinted upon the very functioning of the universe. In Jesus' observation, "Very truly I tell you, unless a kernel of wheat falls to the ground and dies, it remains only a single seed. But if it dies, it produces many seeds."[17] A kernel of wheat will only find its purpose if it gives of itself. It will grow into wheat if it is willing to no longer be a kernel.

The cycle of nature is based on death giving way to life and on self-giving as the logic that generates further life.

A fundamental quality of existence is that it is *given*. It is offered for free, and it is multiplied when we extend it further. Grace is the environment in which life flourishes. Nature gives of itself, we receive from all around, and by receiving, we learn the basic posture of giving back. That's because our Creator is a self-giving God. He gave us life in creation, and he gave us his new life when he gave of himself on the cross. As Bernard of Clairvaux expresses poetically, "In the first act he gave me myself; in the second he gave himself; and when he did that he gave me back myself. Given and given back, I owe myself in return for myself, twice over."[18]

The dynamic of self-giving is not merely Jesus' centuries-old advice. It is our participation in the way God functions and in the logic he imprinted on reality. As a theologian has put it, "All finite beings exist because of God's giving-away; and it bears the marks of its origin, because *in the scheme of finite reality all things give themselves to be known and loved*." In other words, God's self-giving nature is imprinted on everything he created. "[We are] always, we could say, moving towards being seen, being understood and delighted in ... moving out of itself at every level and in every mode."[19] In Hans Urs von Balthasar's analysis, God's giving-away on the cross is the pattern behind all reality. It is the mode in which our souls function, the "prototype of everything."[20]

If this observation is correct, God's logic of self-giving lies behind not only the functioning of the universe, but it is also written upon our hearts. For behind all our efforts of self-centeredness, all our paraphernalia of self-service, lies this. For the glimpse of a moment we present ourselves to the other, we offer ourselves as a possible gift, and we wait to be appreciated, known, and loved. This is what we long for with all our ambitions and pursuits—the very thing we try to achieve through self-centeredness. We accrue reputation, attractiveness, and hard work in the hope of being a gift worthy of being received. We are so preoccupied with the self because the self is the gift we have to offer to the world, the only shot we have at entering the dance of self-giving, appreciation, and love. We constantly offer of ourselves to one another, every day, every time we meet someone or imagine meeting someone. This is what makes us risk raising our eyes to someone crossing our path and offering a glance, waiting to be looked at in return. This is what motivates us to work hard in the expectation that a select group of people will look at our legacy and say, "Well done." We present ourselves to one another. The whole of our lives aims to be a grand, wholehearted gift. Made in the image of God, we follow him in our deepest desires. We give ourselves and long to receive others in return.

This dance of mutual self-giving is the logic that grants our lives meaning before God and others. The measure of our giving is the measure of our significance. We are defined not by how much we get but by how much we share. We feel in our deepest instincts that the ultimate purpose of living is not self-contained. Even the most egocentric of persons craves to leave something behind. In moments of departure, and when the final deathbed departure comes, we long to have offered our beings to others, to have been worthy gifts. And we long most of all for that unimaginable embrace, that everlasting satisfaction, which will be God's smile upon receiving us to himself.

THE RHYTHM OF LOVE

This rhythm of being can be expressed in one word central to Jesus, the Scriptures, and Jesus' followers: love. For the word love refers to the action by which we transcend self-centeredness to encounter someone and give of ourselves. It is the dynamic where we meet and are met, where we know and are known. Love is the aim of self-giving—the atmosphere resulting from the mutual offering of persons to one another. Without self-denial there is no genuine move outward; without self-giving there is no true encounter. When we love we offer our beings to one another, forgetting ourselves amidst affection.[21]

With his call to self-denial and self-giving, Jesus is inviting us to the logic he would express later as loving God and loving neighbor as oneself, for love is the impulse that generates self-denial and self-giving. That's why people who fall in love feel they live for the other and receive life from the other. It's why they promise to be together in sickness and in health and commit to take care of someone as they do of themselves. Love is the voluntary, delightful movement of self-denial in order to give of ourselves.

And here lies a fundamental truth: In love we get *when we give*. We encounter when we give of ourselves. Giving is a precondition for getting. If we do not open ourselves to the other, there won't be an encounter or the possibility of love. We won't receive anything unless we step into the dance of giving and receiving.

But when we dare step outward, look beyond ourselves, and cherish the presence of others, we find what we have been searching for all along: the dynamic of love. We give and receive in a mutual offering of surrender. We delight in one another; we savor the encounter of souls that make space to receive the other. Love arrives as the greatest reward, as the deepest pleasure of our search for happiness. As Bernard of Clairvaux puts it, love "is its own merit, its own reward. Love has no cause or fruit beyond itself: its fruit is its use. I love because I love. I love that I may love."[22]

Love is, so to speak, the last skin of the onion: It is the fulfillment of what it means to be a person, the inner dynamic we search for in general terms as happiness. We live so we can love. We find meaning for existence in the grand offering of ourselves to others. The appreciation we find in love is what we long for behind our pursuits, behind even the most self-centered of actions. And love, by its very nature, is predicated on denial and giving of the self.

Love is the final puzzle piece to understand Jesus' paradox. The saving life by losing life paradigm, which sounds illogical and incomprehensible at first, shows here its core mechanism. Love, the ultimate dynamic we search for in vain through self-centeredness, is experienced successfully when we enter its own logic and give of ourselves. The desperate urge for getting is satisfied when our functioning is based instead on giving. We renounce everything to receive everything; we share of ourselves to find ourselves; we forget about our happiness to receive it unexpectedly.[23] We find the plenitude we try to grasp by saving life when we lose it. We get by giving. The happiness we long for will be found—coming now full circle—when we deny ourselves, take up our crosses, and follow Jesus.

CHAPTER 8
Living Jesus' Happiness

W hen a young man set himself on fire in Tunisia in 2010, nobody could have foreseen the magnitude of the consequences. A wave of protests took multitudes to the streets there and in neighboring Egypt. In both countries, long-time dictators finally gave in. Masses also opposed regimes in Libya, Syria, Bahrain, and Yemen, only to receive cruel responses from their governments. Political instability hit Morocco, Lebanon, Jordan, and Oman. A protracted civil war took place in Syria and displaced millions of people.

One of the most dramatic events of the early twenty-first century has been the wave of revolutions that shook regimes and dethroned governments in North Africa and the Middle East: the Arab Spring. Protestors took to the streets against regimes in varied contexts and with different kinds of proposals, but there was an interesting common factor: the number of years the leaders of those countries had been in power. Hosni Mubarak, for example, had been president of Egypt for thirty years when he finally left office in 2011. In 2011, Ben Ali had been in power for twenty-three years in Tunisia; Ali Abdullah Saleh had ruled for thirty-three years in Yemen; Gaddafi had held power for forty-one years in Libya. Many of these countries were ruled for decades by the same leaders.

In South Africa, however, Nelson Mandela left behind a different kind of legacy. His presidency was celebrated as a victory for the majority black population, and he received the Nobel Peace Prize. But maybe Mandela's most enduring legacy—more consequential than any feat as president—will be that he left power voluntarily. Mandela could have stayed for decades as president; he was beloved in South Africa and had global support. But had he remained in power, in the end he would have been just one more African dictator. Mandela decided to help solidify a lasting democratic regime by leaving office when his term expired and making way for a new president to be elected. Generations later, the words of a leader sound more and more distant. His feats seem more and more remote. But the *model* left by a Mubarak or a Mandela makes a difference. It guides, instructs, and inspires followers decades after their days of glory.

The model we have of the paradox of happiness could not be more captivating. It could not be clearer or more convincing. Jesus is at once the happiest of us all and the one least concerned with his own happiness. He is the embodiment of self-denial and the ideal of human expression. He is the universe's pulse of self-giving, who emptied himself to the point of the cross, but who received everything at his feet. Jesus is our model, our way, and our life. Here we meet the teacher we are to follow, the person whose self-giving we receive and carry on, the living expression of the paradox of happiness.

THE PARADOX OF HAPPINESS

Before we conclude with the final element of Jesus' call—to follow him along his cruciform path—it is helpful to review the terrain we have explored so far.

The human being has an undeniable hunger for happiness. It's a legitimate quest, since we were created by a jubilant God so we could enjoy his plenitude. Our common approaches to happiness try to satisfy this hunger in ways that do not take into account the turned-in nature of our souls, which have been curved by sin, and that are not able to avoid the self-centered logic by which we function. These approaches propose variations of a plastic form of happiness—equated to pleasure, divorced from the ethical texture of life, and wrapped in attractive consumer products. Although following different paths, these proposals do not go beyond self-centeredness. To start with the self is to end with nothing but the self, and a miserable one.

Happiness is an indirect by-product, however. It comes as a consequence of correctly enjoying life. We are happy not when we are obsessed with our emotional state, but when, immersed in some activity, relationship, or cause, we surrender to life in self-forgetfulness. Only when we transcend the prison of the self do we enlarge our souls to savor the full breadth of life's delights.

The dynamic of happiness is also paradoxical because life was not created for the selfish fruition of each man for himself, but as a dynamic of mutuality and love. Reality functions according to a generous logic—after the pattern of the gracious community of persons which is God, and after the supreme act of self-giving by which Jesus offered himself and thus redeemed the world. This dynamic of life shapes the way our hearts function in their deepest desires: We long to present ourselves to one another, to be gifts to one another. We wish to know and be known, cherished, and appreciated. What we pursue behind all we do, even in bent-in ways, is to give of ourselves.

Jesus' paradox thus expresses a fundamental truth of human existence and of our search for happiness: We save our lives when we lose them. To give of ourselves is the essence of what we long to do; it is what grants meaning to our lives before God and one another. In this way, Jesus' call—to deny ourselves, take up our cross, and follow him—is his invitation to join in his dynamic fullness of life. If we are surprised by happiness when we forget it, then we will be happy when we assume a self-giving posture and live for Jesus, our model, way, and life for a paradoxically joyous existence.

JESUS IS OUR MODEL, OUR WAY, AND OUR LIFE

Jesus is our model because denial of ourselves and taking up our crosses are just the manners through which we fulfill the call's true purpose: to follow Jesus.[1] These postures qualify what a lifetime of following Jesus implies; they describe the terrain we cross to walk after him. Jesus' call to discipleship may sound difficult to fulfill, but as Caesarius of Arles noted in the second century, "To what place are we to follow Christ if not where he has already gone?"[2] If we lose clarity of what denying ourselves and taking up our crosses look like, we have Jesus as a model to emulate. If we lose courage to pursue this paradoxical path, he is there to show us the joy waiting at the end. He is our example of what it means to orientate our being to God, to stretch our soul straight in a cruciform embrace of the world, and to live by giving of ourselves to one another. He's the embodiment of gaining life by losing it, of getting through giving. We learn who we are to be by knowing who Jesus is.

Jesus is also our way, for our cruciform posture and discipleship take place not just after him, but also *with* him. We participate in Jesus' own life, self-denial and self-giving.[3] We bear his wounds and share in his glory (Rom 8:17). As we relate to Jesus, his being becomes the way—the avenue, so to speak—on which we transit: we live in Christ, and Christ lives in us. As Paul expressed it, "I have been crucified with Christ and I no longer live, but Christ lives in me. The life I now live in the body, I live by faith in the Son of God, who loved me and gave himself for me" (Gal 2:20). The self-denial and self-giving we can muster are feeble at best, and do not have life within themselves. But we are called to participate in Jesus' own cruciform offering to the world, and here we are united to the grand flow that shapes the universe, to the movement of the cross, to the eternal fountain of goodness and happiness. The logic that reengineers our beings is the logic of Christ himself being poured into us and spilling over for the benefit of people around us. Jesus comes to us in selflessness and generosity; he meets others through us in the resulting posture of self-denial and self-giving.

Jesus is also our life—the one after whom, with whom, yet also by whom we live. The life that energizes us is Christ's; the acuteness of benevolence needed to reverse our proneness to self-centeredness day by day is also his. Just as a branch plucked out of a tree would wither and die, so would our efforts to follow Jesus' cruciform way fail without his presence to sustain and feed us (John 15:5). Yet we can count on the resolution of all paradoxes at work in us: the Son of Man, who makes us sons of God; the one who descended to prepare an ascent for us; the one who swallows our mortality within his immortality, our weakness in his strength, our poverty in his richness, our iniquity in his righteousness, and our self-centeredness in his eternal offering of self-giving.[4]

The one who gained his life by losing it is he who gives us life. The one whose sacrifice cost all yet gave him everything is the one who gives of himself once more through us. The riddle of the ages, the embodiment of contradictions, the manifestations of paradoxes in one divine, blameless life is the Jesus we follow. For him we forsake everything; for him we pour out our very beings. We would not have a doubt if we were to choose between Jesus and our personal happiness. And that's why our hearts are filled, why our faces burst out in laughter, why our souls stand and sing and dance, because for him we lose everything, and gain everything, and march along the cruciform path as the happiest of all.

Acknowledgments

I would like to thank some people who, living generously, gave of themselves to me and contributed to my formation as a person and to the writing of this book. Thank you to my parents, Gunther e Lorití, and my siblings Lory e Rony, for loving me and helping me cultivate generosity and prune my self-centeredness throughout the years. Thanks to André Fontana for detecting and nurturing the life of Christ in me, and to Diogo Andrade, Rafael Costa, and Rafael Faria for giving of themselves to me in friendship for so many years.

I would like to thank also Darrell Johnson and Rikk Watts, whose passion for Jesus has molded me and helped me form a Christocentric understanding of life and of happiness. Thanks to Josué Campanhã for making the first edition of this work possible, and to Cinthia Oliveira Simas and Osmar Ludovico, who have read different portions of the manuscript and offered suggestions for improvement. Elizabeth Vince and Ryan Rotz at Kirkdale Press were attentive and efficient partners in the publication of the first edition of this book.

A final thank you to my beloved Sarah for encouraging me to write, for so many brilliant suggestions, and for giving yourself to me so openly and generously. Thank you.

Notes

CHAPTER I: PLASTIC HAPPINESS

1. Pascal Bruckner, *A Euforia Perpétua: Ensaio Sobre o Dever da Felicidade* [Perpetual euphoria: on the duty to be happy], trans. Rejane Janowitzer (Rio de Janeiro: Bertrand, 2002), 16, 74, 77.

2. Blaise Pascal, *The Mind on Fire: A Faith for the Skeptical and Indifferent*, ed. James M. Houston (Vancouver: Regent College Publishing, 1989), 108.

3. Ibid.

4. Alexander Pope, quoted in Darrin M. McMahon, *Happiness: A History* (New York: Grove Press, 2006), 200.

5. Sigmund Freud, *Civilization and Its Discontents*, trans. James Strachey (New York: W. W. Norton, 1962), 26.

6. Augustine, quoted in John Piper, *Desiring God: Meditations of a Christian Hedonist* (Sisters, OR: Multnomah, 2003), 52.

7. John 10:10.

8. Martin Luther, quoted in Darrin McMahon, *Happiness*, 165.

9. Jonathan Edwards is a representative theologian who grounds the human search for happiness in God's being and in God's creation of humans in his image: "God may have a real and proper pleasure or happiness in seeing the happy state of the creature: yet this may not be different from his delight in himself; being a delight in his own infinite goodness; of the exercise of that glorious propensity of his nature to diffuse and communicate himself, and so gratifying this inclination of his own heart." Jonathan Edwards, "End of Creation," in *The Works of Jonathan Edwards*, vol. 8, ed. Perry Miller (New Haven: Yale University Press, 1957), 446.

10. Isaiah 66:10–14; Revelation 21:4

11. In my estimation, our reticence to address happiness from a Christian perspective is what produced our half-conscious pursuit of happiness as defined outside of the Christian framework, as well as theologies controlled by worldly notions of happiness, such as the health and wealth gospel.

12. Matthew 5:18, Aristotle, quoted in Darrin McMahon, *Happiness*, 45.

13. Thomas Aquinas, as quoted in Pat Killion Coate, *The Little Book of Happiness: Quotes by History's Icons, Celebrities, and Saints* (Charleston, SC: BookSurge Publishing, 2006).

14. Epicurus and John Locke, quoted in Darrin McMahon, *Happiness*, 54, 181.

15. Jeremy Bentham, quoted in Ibid., 212.
16. Sigmund Freud, *Civilization and Its Discontents*, 29.
17. Julien Offray de la Mettrie, in Darrin MacMahon, *Happiness*, 228.

CHAPTER TWO: THE SPECTRUM OF POSSIBILITIES

1. Ernest Hemingway, quoted in Daniel M. Haybron, *The Pursuit of Unhappiness: The Elusive Psychology of Well-Being* (Oxford and New York: Oxford University Press, 2008), 108.
2. Epicterus, in Ibid., 54.
3. Søren Kierkegaard, "Either/Or, A Fragment of Life, I," in *The Essential Kierkegaard*, ed. Howard V. Hong and Edna H. Hong (Princeton: Princeton University Press, 2000), 40.
4. Marquise du Châtelet, in Darrin MacMahon, *Happiness*, 202.
5. Martin Luther, quoted in Matt Jenson, *The Gravity of Sin: Augustine, Luther and Barth on Homo Incurvatus In Se* (London and New York: T & T Clark, 2006), 70. Luther famously defines sin as an essential incurvature unto ourselves: "Our nature has been so deeply curved in upon itself because of the viciousness of original sin that it not only turns the finest gifts of God in upon itself and enjoys them (as is evident in the case of legalists and hypocrites), indeed, it even uses God Himself to achieve these aims, but it also seems to be ignorant of this very fact, that in acting so iniquitously, so perversely, and in such a depraved way, it is even seeking God for its own sake." Luther, in ibid., 81. Blaise Pascal is another theologian who defines sin as curvedness unto oneself. "For if we were born reasonable and impartial, with a knowledge of ourselves and of others, we would not have this bias toward ourselves in our own wills. But we are born with it, and so we are born perverted. Everything tends toward itself, and this is contrary to order." Blaise Pascal, *The Mind on Fire*, 66.
6. Augustine, quoted in Kenneth Boa, *Augustine to Freud: What Theologians & Psychologists Tell Us about Human Nature [And Why It Matters]* (Nashville: Broadman & Holman, 2004), 8.
7. Karl Barth, quoted in Matt Jenson, *The Gravity of Sin*, 173.
8. Matt Jenson develops this point in theological language. "'Fleshly' man is man as he attempts to live in pure self-relation, with all other potential relationships being instrumentally collapsed into the self-relation. Carnal man, we might say, asserts a gravitational pull on all around him and lives centripetally. ... [But] this God-self relation relativizes the spiritual man and continually draws him out of himself ecstatically, as he finds his life in Christ and then in his neighbour. Thus, homo spiritualis lives centrifugally and eccentrically." Ibid., 66.
9. Blaise Pascal, *The Mind on Fire*, 217.
10. Karl Barth, quoted in Matt Jenson, *The Gravity of Sin*, 173.

CHAPTER THREE: A PARADOXICAL CALL

1. Augustine, *The Confessions of St. Augustine*, ed. and trans. Albert Cook Outler (Mineola, NY: Dover, 2002), V.XIII–XIV.
2. Ibid., IX.I.1.

3. Ibid., I.IV.4.

4. 2 Corinthians 13:9; 1 Corinthians 1:25; Galatians 5:13; 1 Peter 1:6, 8; Luke 18:22; Matthew 11:29.

5. Matthew 5:3, 5.

6. 2 Corinthians 6:9–10.

7. W. K. Stewart, quoted in Narry S. Santos, *Slave of All: The Paradox of Authority and Servanthood in the Gospel of Mark, Journal for the Study of the New Testament: Supplement Series 237* (London: Sheffield Academic Press, 2003), 14.

8. We start here to investigate Mark 8:35 and proceed in Part Three to Mark 8:34. The "for" in Mark 8:35 shows that this sentence is the reason for the one preceding it.

9. Mark 4:12.

10. Mark 9:35; 10:31, 44–45; Matthew 23:12.

11. Lamar Williamson Jr. situates the centrality of this passage when he affirms, "First, [Mark 8:27–9:1] is the geographical and theological fulcrum at the mid-point of Mark. ... The public ministry in Galilee is essentially finished; from this point onward the action is directed toward Jerusalem. The question of Jesus' identity is here answered by Peter's confession that he is the Christ (v. 29), and immediately the theological focus shifts to what it means for Jesus to be Christ (v. 31) and for his followers to be Christians (v. 34), themes which will dominate the remainder of the Gospel. Second, this is the opening, thematic passage in the body of Mark's section on discipleship." Lamar Williamson Jr., *Mark*, Interpretation (Atlanta: John Knox Press, 1983), 150.

12. Only after the disciples hear about the way of the cross and what it means to their lives are they prepared for the next revelation of Jesus' identity: the transfiguration (Mark 9). They first need to know the cross so they can correctly interpret Jesus' glory.

13. "M. E. Boring ... takes 'the crowd' in v 34 as Mark's addition to include the church in Jesus' audience. But Mark's redaction shows that he has an even wider audience in view: the crowd represents non-Christians, summoned to Christian discipleship." R. H. Gundry, *Mark: A Commentary on His Apology for the Cross* (Grand Rapids: Eerdmans, 1993), 452. In addition, the general formulas "anyone" in Mark 8:34, "whoever" in Mark 8:35 (twice) and Mark 8:38, and "man" in Mark 8:36, 37 also emphasize the universality of Jesus' call here. R. T. France, *The Gospel of Mark*, NIGTC (Grand Rapids/Cambridge, U.K.: Eerdmans; Carlisle: Paternoster, 2002), 339.

14. John 10:10.

15. Mark 8:35.

16. Robert C. Tannehill, *The Sword of His Mouth* (Philadelphia: Fortress Press, 1975), 99–100.

17. John Stott, *The Cross of Christ* (Downers Grove: InterVarsity Press, 1986), 279.

18. Luke 9:23.

19. The task of this book is to extract the implications of Jesus' words in this passage for our quest for happiness. For a straightforward, more thorough exposition of Mark 8:34–37 and its context, see one of the commentaries quoted, especially R. T. France, *The Gospel of Mark*, NIGTC (Grand Rapids/Cambridge, U.K.: Eerdmans; Carlisle: Paternoster, 2002), 331–345. Two other

balanced, quality commentaries are Craig, A. Evans, *Mark 8:27–16:20*, WBC 34B (Nashville: Thomas Nelson, 2001); and Morna D. Hooker, *The Gospel According to St. Mark*, BNTC (London: A. & C. Black, 1991). For an extensive examination of technical issues, see R. H. Gundry, *Mark: A Commentary on His Apology for the Cross* (Grand Rapids: Eerdmans, 1993).

CHAPTER FOUR: THE GIFT OF HAPPINESS

1. Jean-Jacques Rousseau, quoted in Darrin MacMahon, *Happiness*, 241.

2. Arthur Schopenhauer, quoted in Armand M. Nicholi Jr., *The Question of God: C. S. Lewis and Sigmund Freud Debate God, Love, Sex and the Meaning of Life* (New York: Free Press, 2002), 98.

3. Neil Clark Warren, *Finding Contentment* (Nashville: Thomas Nelson, 1997), 34.

4. Gregory of Nyssa, *From Glory to Glory*, ed. Jean Danielou (Crestwood, NY: St. Vladimir's Press, 1961), 87–88.

5. Bernard of Clairvaux, *On Loving God, and Selections from His Sermons*, ed. Hugh Martin (London: SCM Press, 1959), 69.

6. Sigmund Freud, *Civilization and Its Discontents*, 30.

7. Malcolm Muggeridge, "Happiness," in *Jesus Rediscovered* (Bungay: Collins, 1969), 146.

8. I owe this example to a similar one used in Mark Vernon, *Wellbeing* (Stockfield: Acumen, 2008), 4.

9. Ralph W. Sockman, *The Paradoxes of Jesus* (New York: Abingdon Press, 1936), 232.

10. Edith Wharton, quoted in Pat Killion Coate, *The Little Book of Happiness*, 77.

11. W. Beran Wolfe, quoted in Ibid.

12. John Stuart Mill, *Autobiography and Other Writings*, ed. Jack Stillinger (Boston: Houghton Mifflin Company, 1969), 85.

13. Mark Vernon, *Wellbeing*, 3.

14. Ibid., 34.

15. Viktor E. Frankl, *Man's Search for Meaning* (New York: Washington Square Press, 1984), 16–17.

16. Mark Vernon, *Wellbeing*, 48.

17. John Stuart Mill, *Autobiography*, 85.

18. Chuang Tzu, quoted in Pat Killion Coate, *The Little Book of Happiness*, 17, 19.

19. Marvin C. Shaw, *The Paradox of Intention: Reaching the Goal by Giving Up the Attempt to Reach It* (Atlanta: Scholar's Press, 1988), 5.

20. Nathaniel Hawthorne, quoted in Daniel Nettle, *Happiness: The Science Behind Your Smile* (Oxford and New York: Oxford University Press, 2005), 184.

21. James M. Houston, *The Fulfillment: Pursuing True Happiness* (Colorado Springs: Victor, 2007), 16.

22. Ralph Sockman, *The Paradoxes of Jesus*, 243.

CHAPTER FIVE: BEYOND THE RULE OF THE SELF

1. Vincent van Gogh, as quoted in the description of the painting in the Museum of Modern Art in New York.

2. H. R. Rookmaaker, *Modern Art & the Death of a Culture* (Downers Grove: InterVarsity Press, 1970), 94.

3. Mike Martin, "Paradoxes of Happiness," 173.

4. Matt Jenson, *The Gravity of Sin*, 73.

5. Malcolm Muggeridge, "Happiness," *Jesus Rediscovered*, 147.

6. C. S. Lewis, quoted in Ed René Kivitz, *Vivendo com Propósitos: A Resposta Cristã ao Sentido da Vida [Living with purpose: the Christian answer to the meaning of life]* (São Paulo: Mundo Cristão, 2003), 93.

7. Pascal, *The Mind on Fire*, 95.

CHAPTER SIX: OPENING UP TO LIFE

1. "'Losing one's life' must be understood in the sense of denying oneself, taking up one's cross, and following Jesus, as referred to in 8:34." Robert H. Stein, *Mark*, BECNT (Grand Rapids: Baker Academic, 2008), 408. The meaning of losing life for Jesus and the gospel is implied in the context: denying oneself, taking up one's cross, and following Jesus. Adela Yarbro Collins, *Mark: A Commentary*, Hermeneia (Minneapolis: Fortress Press, 2007), 376.

2. This perspective is framed by Matthew the Poor, a monk with a lifetime of experience in ascetic practices. "We should not see austerity, or asceticism, as an end in itself. Neither should we delight in practicing it to the exclusion of everything else. By doing so we are only allowing it to distract us from progressing toward God and completing our union with him in mature love. ... Ascetic disciplines are nothing more than the means to mortify the old Adam and crucify our will, our passions, and the desires that work in us for iniquity. Ascesis is only a way of showing our love and tender feelings toward God." Matthew the Poor, *Orthodox Prayer Life: The Interior Way* (Crestwood: St Vladimir's Seminary Press, 2003), 118.

3. C. S. Lewis, *The Screwtape Letters* (New York: HarperOne, 2001), 70.

4. John Stott, *The Cross of Christ*, 282. Andrew Wall's insight about the conversion of cultures to Christ helps illuminate the dynamic of self-denial as well: a movement which "is not about substitution, the replacement of something old for something new, but about transformation, the turning of the already existing to new account." Andrew Walls, "The Translation Principle in Christian History," in *The Missionary Movement in Christian History: Studies in the Transmission of Faith* (Maryknoll: Orbis; Edinburgh: T&T Clark, 1996), 28.

5. John Calvin, *Institutes of Christian Religion*, trans. Henry Beveridge (Peabody: Hendrickson, 2008), III.vii.1.

6. C. S. Lewis, *The Weight of Glory* (New York: HarperCollins, 1980), 26.

7. Bernard of Clairvaux, *Selected Works*, ed. Emilie Griffin (San Francisco: HarperOne, 2005), 67.

8. My view aligns with that of Augustine and Bernard of Clairvaux, who approved the love of self for God's sake. Martin Luther, on the other hand, rejected every form of self-love. "You are completely curved in upon yourself

and pointed toward love of yourself, a condition from which you will not be delivered unless you altogether cease loving yourself and, forgetting yourself, love your neighbor. ... Either one seeks one's own in everything, even in one's neighbour, forgetting all others but oneself, or one forgets oneself and seeks the good of one's neighbour in everything." Martin Luther, quoted in Matt Jenson, *The Gravity of Sin*, 90.

9.   Étienne Gilson, *The Mystical Theology of St. Bernard*, trans. A. H. C. Downes (Kalamazoo, MI: Cistercian Publications, 1990), 142–145.

10.   Dietrich Bonhoeffer, quoted in Stott, *The Cross of Christ*, 279.

11.   C. S. Lewis, *Mere Christianity* (New York: HarperOne, 2001), 196–197, 227.

CHAPTER SEVEN: GETTING BY GIVING

1.   Julian, quoted in Rodney Stark, *The Rise of Christianity: How the Obscure, Marginal Jesus Movement Became the Dominant Religious Force in the Western World in a Few Centuries* (New York: HarperOne, 1996), 84.

2.   Ibid., 189.

3.   "There is an intimate connection between Christology and discipleship in the Gospel of Mark. Both meet at the cross. Just as one cannot understand who Jesus is apart from the cross, so one cannot grasp the true meaning of discipleship unless he or she is willing to follow Jesus 'on the way.' That way, of course, leads to the cross." F. Matera, quoted in Narry Santos, *Slave of All*, 17.

4.   We are not to interpret the phrase "made himself nothing" as if Jesus repressed or annihilated his own self. Even at the humblest of stages, Jesus was still God in human form, amazing his audiences with his love and wisdom, though with striking humility. The phrase "made himself nothing" should rather be interpreted in the lines we have been following in this chapter. He made his own self nothing; he removed his self from sight so as to not live for himself. The self as the selfish god we live for—that was nothing for Jesus.

5.   Michael J. Gorman, *Cruciformity: Paul's Narrative Spirituality of the Cross* (Grand Rapids: Eerdmans, 2001), 170, 174.

6.   Calvin, *Institutes*, III.viii.1.

7.   Matthew Henry, *Matthew Henry's Commentary on the Whole Bible: Complete and Unabridged in One Volume* (Peabody: Hendrickson, 1996), S. Mt 16:24.

8.   Gilbert K. Chesterton, *Orthodoxy* (Vancouver: Regent College Publishing, 2004), 109.

9.   Williamson, *Mark*, 154.

10.   Martin Luther, *The Freedom of a Christian*, ed. Mark D. Tranvik (Minneapolis: Fortress Press, 2008), 48. Luther's full quote is: "A man does not live for himself alone in this mortal body to work for it alone, but he lives also for all men on earth; rather, he lives only for others and not for himself." While I agree with the substance of Luther's others-oriented ethic, I disagree that the biblical ethic excludes in absolute terms living for oneself. Jesus' command is not to love others and cease loving ourselves; rather, we are to love others as we love ourselves.

11. Rowan Williams, quoted in Miroslav Volf, *Exclusion & Embrace: A Theological Exploration of Identity, Otherness, and Reconciliation* (Nashville: Abingdon Press, 1996), 127.

12. Ibid., 129.

13. Dallas Willard, quoted in Richard Foster, *Celebration of Discipline* (Edinburgh: Hodder, 1996), 357.

14. Leonardo Boff, quoted in Stanley Grenz, *Rediscovering the Triune God: The Trinity in Contemporary Theology* (Minneapolis: Fortress Press, 2004), 125. Similarly, Grenz describes Thomas Torrance's triune theology in the follow way: "In his estimation, the loving, communion-establishing God who encounters humans in Christ is the one who is eternally relational because of the eternal indwelling and communion of the three trinitarian persons within the inner dynamic of the triune God." Ibid., 213.

15. Ibid., 138.

16. Ibid., 139; Thomas F. Torrance, quoted in ibid., 214.

17. John 12:24.

18. Bernard of Clairvaux, *Selected Works*, ed. Emilie Griffin (San Francisco: HarperOne, 2005), 65.

19. Rowan Williams, "Balthasar and the Trinity," in *The Cambridge Companion to Hans Urs von Balthasar*, ed. Edward Oakes and David Moss (Cambridge: Cambridge University Press, 2004), 41. Emphasis added.

20. Ibid.

21. Ralph Sockman, *The Paradoxes of Jesus*, 248.

22. Bernard of Clairvaux, quoted in Bernard McGinn, *The Growth of Mysticism* (New York: Crossroad, 1994), 199.

23. Kierkegaard describes the movement of renouncing everything to yet receive it as the "paradoxical movement of faith." Søren Kierkegaard, "Fear and Trembling," in *The Essential Kierkegaard*, 98.

CHAPTER EIGHT: LIVING JESUS' HAPPINESS

1. Lamar Williamson, *Mark*, 154.

2. Caesarius of Arles, quoted in Thomas C. Oden and Christopher A. Hall, eds., *Mark*, Ancient Christian Commentary on Scripture, New Testament II (Downers Grove: InterVarsity Press, 1998), 113.

3. John McLeod Campbell describes this participation in Christ thus: "Therefore Christ, as the Lord of our spirits and our life, devotes us to God and devotes us to men in the fellowship of his self-sacrifice." John McLeod Campbell, quoted in Andrew Purves, *Reconstructing Pastoral Theology: A Christological Foundation* (Louisville: Westminster John Knox Press, 2004), 53.

4. John Calvin, quoted in Purves, *Reconstructing Pastoral Theology*, 78.